MW01049648

Fundamentalism: A Catholic Perspective

Thomas F. O'Meara, O.P.

Paulist Press ■ New York ■ New Jersey

Material that makes up much of chapter one appeared first in *The Priest* magazine, published by Our Sunday Visitor.

Library of Congress Cataloging-in-Publication Data

O'Meara, Thomas F., 1935–
   Fundamentalism: a Catholic perspective/Thomas F. O'Meara.
     p. cm.
   Includes bibliographical references.
   ISBN 0-8091-3133-1
   1. Fundamentalism—Controversial literature. 2. Catholic Church—
Doctrines. I. Title.
   BT82.2.046   1990
   230'.046—dc20

                                                  89-38558
                                                   CIP

Published by Paulist Press
997 Macarthur Boulevard
Mahwah, N.J. 07430

Printed and bound in the United States of America

Contents

PART TWO: THE CATHOLIC PERSPECTIVE

for
Kathy O'Meara Fryer

Foreword

This is a book for Catholics, not a book against fundamentalists. Fundamentalism, however, implies a rejection, more or less, of others. A narrow and rigid understanding of a religious creed or a political approach will keep its distance from other men and women. Soon the good news can become the bad news, the sad news about others displeasing God in this life and being damned in the next. The exclusivity of any fundamentalist group leads to convert-making, and because Roman Catholics are numerous, they can become the prey of a variety of evangelists and reformers. This book is a guide to the differences between the Catholic view of Christianity and that espoused by Protestant fundamentalists.

But, as the opening chapters show, there are also observations on the extent of fundamentalism—reaching to Islam and Marxism, or to American politics—and brief treatments of a fundamentalist theology within Catholicism itself.

This book is more about Catholicism than fundamentalism. It is necessary not simply because Catholics, in an age of change but also opportunity, can find fundamentalisms seductive, but because Catholicism in its approach to Christian life, worship, church and culture is the polar opposite of every fundamentalism, Christian or other.

The following pages express two of the author's theological interests: how the gospel becomes incarnate in different cultures and historical eras, and the relationship of grace to the human personality.

PART ONE

The Fundamentalist Believer

1

Fundamentalism and Our Times

"You don't cut no corners with the Bible!"
CHRISTIAN SNAKE-HANDLER
IN WEST VIRGINIA

"Men will say: Bible days are here again!"
JIMMY SWAGGART

Television brings us newscasts and soap operas, sports events and talk-shows. But television also brings us religion. On dozens of cable systems televangelists offer daily gospels and miracles live and in color. Who would have forecast twenty-five years ago that the contemporary and two-dimensional world of TV would transmit dozens of shows about faiths, ministries and revelations? And, after the recent escapades of fundamentalist televangelists, some wonder: Is all religion either a neurosis or a confidence game? Oral Roberts ascended to his prayer tower to negotiate the price of his life; Jim and Tammy Bakker withdrew to the desert (in this case, Palm Springs) as their city shoddily built and left unfinished—where all would be "nice for God"—collapsed financially. Jimmy Swaggart's prophecies condemned millions of people weeks before his visits to a New Orleans prostitute were reported. Famous and wealthy television evangelists moved from starring on cable TV to enacting the pro-wrestling of American religion.

The fundamentalist mood is wider than cable television. We can add to Protestant fundamentalism a list of similar events in other groups: weeping ikons in Greek Orthodox churches; photographs of the Blessed Virgin Mary appearing in New Jersey and the Philippines; calls by some Catholics, lay and clergy, to denounce all liturgy beyond the Latin mass; propaganda for South Africa and Israel that they are divinely approved while their neighbors are cursed; decrees from Iran that novelists or women intellectuals are to be executed. Religion and faith seem to have gone mad, and contrary to the expectations of secular intellectuals this religious attitude is everywhere.

> The issues involved in fundamentalism are without doubt among the most serious pastoral problems for the church of today. Very many people are seriously concerned with them. . . . The alienation between people that it brings about is extreme. Lay people come to regard their minister as "unsound" or worse. Within families it is common for young persons brought up in a Christian home to become fundamentalists and to end up evaluating their devoted upbringing as little better than paganism. Irreconcilable religious tension between husband and wife sometimes leads to the verge of marital breakdown.[1]

Fundamentalism's prominence has for some years been a puzzle and a challenge to Catholics.

We should recall that fundamentalism—*Time* called it "America's great folk faith"—is, of course, not the same as Protestant Christianity. From the great churches of the reformation, Roman Catholics have learned much in an ecumenical spirit over the past twenty-five years. (If Martin Luther were watching Robert Schuller or Leonard Angley he might throw an ink bottle at his television set.)

Christian fundamentalism in America is a collection of church movements not more than one hundred and fifty years old of American origin and membership. Reaching prominence after World War I, they combine theological attitudes toward the Bible, Jesus, the cross, the supernatural and sin with American attitudes about success, certitude, history and respectability. There are differences among evangelicals, charismatics and proper fundamentalists in church and theology. "Evangelicals," the original word for Luther's church, is in the United States an umbrella term for Protestants who stress conservative doctrine and practice. This can encompass many groups with a range of theological and political views. Not all evangelicals are fundamentalists, but many theological principles of the two orientations are similar. "Pentecostals" add to their literal interpretation of the Bible the miraculous, particularly speaking in tongues, prophesying about the future, and healing diseases and deformities. "Fundamentalists" are not described solely by their allegiance to a literal or inerrant scripture (which, to some degree, most traditional Christians would hold) but by an interpretation of the Bible which is rigidly and excessively literal. They misunderstand the poetry in the Hebrew scriptures, the metaphorical in the New Testament. They do not see how God's word is presented differently in stories, parables, and narratives. And they ignore or deny the Bible's complex mix of history and religious message.

If we want to understand this movement with its various branches, we cannot stay with the Bible but need to reach the aspects of faith and psychology which lie beneath this attitude to scripture. What is your image of God? How active is evil in the world? Will the world end violently and soon? Does God want the founding evangelist to fashion Christianity anew? Are conversions always dramatic, and miracles frequent?

Fundamentalist groups and their preachers share common characteristics, and to the extent that movements, theologies, small churches or television programs own these general characteristics, they enter into the subject of our critique. They do not just have an individualist attitude toward scripture: different theologies of God and grace, of Christ and humanity lie beneath the Bible glibly cited. All generally fundamentalist groups have a tradition and an orientation which is somewhat anti-Catholic in its understanding of human nature, sacraments, tradition and church authority. If we are critical of fundamentalist theology, we are not contemptuous of the people who find good things in it: a proclamation of the reality of God in Jesus Christ, a real history of God's work in the Bible, the presence of grace, a fight with evil.

Growing Fundamentalism

In Florida it is estimated that five Catholics enter fundamentalist churches every day. It is said that ten to twenty percent of the monies of Pat Robertson or Jerry Falwell (and earlier of Jimmy Swaggart and Oral Roberts) solicited on television comes from

Catholics. Many Catholic families throughout the country have members who have entered a fundamentalist church of one kind or another. Fr. Richard McBrien in one of his popular columns on this topic observed that the number of Catholics who left the church because of new theological ideas could fit in a phone booth, while the number leaving for fundamentalism would fill stadiums. That particular column received more mail than any other he has written in the past twenty years and prompted serious attention to this issue by the American bishops. New Testament scholar Eugene LaVerdiere writes: "In recent years fundamentalism has been making significant inroads in the Roman Catholic Church, not that we have ever been altogether free of it. Never before, however, have we experienced it in its present form, where Catholics personally opt for a fundamentalist stance towards Scripture and its bearing on Christian life. A committed fundamentalism, as opposed to unconscious fundamentalist influence, is new for us."[2]

Catholicism is invaded by fundamentalisms.

Almost every city with a population of over 150,000 is reached by a radio or television station devoted to fundamentalist programming. The three large religious cable networks, reaching ten to twenty million households, are controlled by fundamentalist groups. Catholics may be giving more money to television's religious evangelists than to their bishops' collections, or to the communities of religious women whose sisters educated and nursed American Catholics for a century. If the media report a decline in contributions to fundamentalist programs on television after the recent sex and money scandals, and if most viewers agree that these programs are too interested in money, still forty-three percent of the viewers think that the devil was involved in Bakker's and Swaggart's difficulties.

Some Catholics may imagine that they will find there a stronger commitment to Christ, a greater certainty about morals. Close examination shows that they also find a different, somewhat hostile Christianity. Jimmy Swaggart wrote a booklet on Catholicism. He mentions his large clientele among Catholics, drawn to him, he says, by the confusion over papal changes and by priests and nuns leaving their vocation. Television is offering Catholics for the first time a chance to hear the word of God. Catholics misunderstand being saved by Christ, the one priesthood of Christ, while they learn little of the Bible because they consider church and tradition also to be sources of revelation. Swaggart argues that every sacrament, every mention of grace, every good work opposes Jesus' salvation. Ultimately Catholicism, like Judaism, because it mentions human activity, is a religion not of faith in Jesus and grace from God but of laws. "Tragically, it is for this same reason that millions of Catholics will die unsaved—because they have been led to believe that through the 'work' of belonging to the Catholic church and participating in the 'sacraments' (which are *nowhere* mentioned in God's Word) that they are 'accepting' Jesus Christ and are therefore saved."[3] Catholics can be saved only by accepting the vocabulary of Jimmy Swaggart; otherwise they are, as on his television programs, to be lumped together with communists and Muslims.

Televised fundamentalism contacts largely older Catholics while door-to-door evangelism proselytizes the large Hispanic populations. Andrew Greeley has offered statistics claiming that 60,000 Catholics of Hispanic origin in the United States are defecting to Protestant denominations each year. Of course, not all of this loss of one million over the past fifteen years is due to fundamentalism (most mainline Protestant churches have a strong investment in converting American Catholic Hispanics), but three quarters are now fundamentalists or Baptists. Greeley's statistics argue that for many becoming a Protestant is a way of becoming middle-class, American, respectable, or of breaking with an old synthesis of Indian Catholicism. At the same time, sects appealingly offer an active and numerous clergy, a personal and emotional faith, a small close-knit church.[4]

We can add to these familiar movements a vivid parade of political fundamentalisms which American Catholics may encounter. These may include followers of Jerry Falwell who equate Christianity with capitalism. "The free enterprise system is clearly outlined in the Book of Proverbs in the Bible. Jesus Christ made it clear that the work ethic was part of His plan for man. Ownership in business is biblical. Ambitious and successful business management is clearly outlined as a part of God's plan for His people."[5] This would leave out of the kingdom of God not only modern Christian socialist politicians at the head of European countries but the general ethos of Mediterranean and Latin lands, any ethos other than that which is Calvinist.

But why such a growth of fundamentalism in the past fifteen years? Churches which provide the miraculous event and the easy answers grow strong in times of uncertain social change. Ministers who find easy scapegoats are popular with people who are threatened by life. Who, twenty-five years ago, would have believed that small, largely southern churches would even exist today, much less be a dominant religious influence through television and politics? University faculties and mainline seminaries then presumed that such churches with their emotional and unscientific forms would have faded away from an increasingly secular and universally liberal America.

Churches of a fundamentalist direction have never been stronger—and they grow! They grow even as most mainline Protestant churches decline by significant numbers every five years. Fundamentalist churches grow by one to two percent a year, while most traditional Protestant churches are declining one half percent to one percent a year. Why this appeal?

They grow because Americans are tired of change: numbed by the past twenty-five years of rapid change in every area of life; frightened by change which leads only to more change. Americans are buffeted by insecurity about money, about the meaning of life, even about existence itself. They are fatigued by crises in meaning, society and morality. Faith should give meaning, orientation and hope; certainly revelation and church should offer more than daily secularism and amoral liberalism.

Today we live like people in a tropical storm; we are hit by questions and problems reported ceaselessly by the media; we live at the heart of the storm with winds coming from all directions. Are surrogate mothers a good idea? How should one view the divorced after a second marriage, or people living together before a marriage? Will reverencing the flag atone for supporting foreign dictators?

It is not only TV which brings fundamentalism into our homes and lives but the people we meet in our daily existence. The dental technician may resolutely explain the death of her brother-in-law (he was electrocuted when the raised trailer of his semi touched a live wire) as simply God's decision that "his time was up"; the retired grandparent may interpret a drought as God's way of condemning negotiations with atheistic Russia; the college junior wonders about the trip his wealthy Catholic parents are making to the latest site of Marian visions.

Fundamentalism is in the air. People respond to fundamentalist theologies and politics. The televised crowds are happy with either an upbeat and simple message, or with an apocalyptic prediction.

Beyond Biblical Shoot-Outs

At first we might think fundamentalism means insisting that a Jew named Jonah lived, Pinocchio-like, in a whale, or that the number of the beast in the New Testament book of Revelation refers to Hitler, Queen Victoria or Libya's Muammer Qaddafi, or that all the galaxies with their billions of suns were formed in one day. Isn't fundamentalism a religion of biblical shoot-outs? Matthew 12:4 eliminates 2 Thessalonians 1:8.

Fundamentalism does have certain attitudes toward the Bible. As we mentioned, this attitude is more than accepting a "literal interpretation," since most Christians want to understand the scriptures as their authors and the Holy Spirit basically intended them to be understood. In the fundamentalist stance, the Bible's narratives are photographed history rather than different kinds of stories with religious messages. Equally important, this preacher or this small church alone has the correct interpretation of God's word, the right view of God and of us.

Fundamentalism, however, tends to focus upon *marginal* issues, e.g., healings, the end of the world, foretelling the future. It often avoids central issues, e.g. how God's grace meets different human lives, or how we make slow political progress toward disarmament or racial justice. Jesus' spoke of detachment and poverty, humility and ordinary charity. Issues of justice and oppression are central to the gospel, but because they are not sensational or easily resolved, not they but disasters and illnesses occupy the evangelist whose radio program we may hear while driving on an autumn evening. Hence the concern of fundamentalist churches to have "the full gospel" lest the right number of answers in the right order of importance be jostled. Eugene LaVerdiere describes their attitude toward scripture.

> For fundamentalists the biblical Word is seen as an absolute, as a reality in itself whose statement is clear and unchanging. It is not relative to the understanding of those who hear it in varying cultural and historical contexts. As a result, it does not require interpretation. In a sense fundamentalism is not a kind of interpretation but a denial of the need and legitimacy of interpretation. It presupposes that the (biblical) Word can be immediately grasped by all. Unwittingly, however, the fundamentalist does interpret. Such is the nature of reading and communication. Without realizing it, the fundamentalist equates the biblical Word with his or her interpretation of it and absolutizes that interpretation as the one interpretation for all.[6]

The biblical word is both human and divine. A fundamentalist stance views the biblical word as a divine word—which it is. In doing so, however, it denies the humanity of the word. Fundamentalism has an apocalyptic view of the human race and its end (one filled with calamity and fear); it describes the world as evil and deserving of a horrible and explosive end filled with suffering men and women. "Contemporary apocalyptic finds little or no hope in the world as we know it . . . (and) fails to recognize the goodness of God's creation."[7]

Archbishop John Whealon observed that Vatican II placed the Bible more in the center of the liturgy and gave scripture a greater presence in all forms of religious education. For Catholics scripture and tradition belong together and together they address issues which are recent and new. "The problem with fundamentalism is that it can give only a few answers, and cannot present those answers in balance. To answer all modern questions from Bible texts is an exercise in astonishing mental gymnastics."[8]

So there can be a critique of fundamentalism from its interpretation of the Hebrew scriptures and the New Testament—but there can also be a critique of its faith and world-view. This book presents the second and goes beyond biblical fundamentalism (with its gospel passages hurled like javelins) to the theological identity and ensemble of fundamentalism. What are the deepest beliefs at work here? What is the psychology of fundamentalism? What is its governing Christian theological attitudes? How does it differ from the Catholic community, theology, worship and ethos?

The Wider Fundamentalism

There is more than Protestant fundamentalism.

There is a Catholic fundamentalism. There is a fundamentalism which invests absolute and certain divine power in a medal. Individual bishops or even Catholic journalists instantly decide who is and who is not obeying this or that papal document. The appearance of the Blessed Virgin in Texas or Yugoslavia (although the local bishops have stated that these claims are without foundation) is more important than faith or charity. We will return to this topic in Chapter 2.

Beyond Christianity, fundamentalism is a worldwide phenomenon. The atmosphere of our times nourishes, like a hothouse, the fundamentalist psyche and movement. Fundamentalisms appear today in political parties as well as in religions; people, like the *Sorcerer's Apprentice,* search for an infallible, supra-human agency to do our bidding, whether this be a store selling magical objects in Spanish Harlem or an expensive spa mixing exercise, pills and biofeedback in California.

The news media describe how fundamentalist clergy determine the course of Iran, how branches of Islam who have been at war for centuries engineer the destruction of Beirut or the intrigues of Libya. On the same Sunday, in Paris or Marseille, there can be banner-filled parades by Marxist workers or by reactionary clergy and laity. One Sunday's parade favors the expulsion of all Arabs and blacks from France, while on the next Sunday the banners held by members of a rigid Islamic sect proclaim that France will eventually be a fundamentalist Islamic state. Bombs are placed in Northern Ireland by an underground which will entertain no political solution other than its own for resolving a situation created by an earlier Presbyterianism which considered the Catholic population to have no rights. The state of Israel has permitted some Jews and some Arabs to reach violent positions where all other human beings except this militant group have, for religious reasons, no identity before God. Santeria, with roots in voodoo, proffers herbs, candles, oils, perfumes and potions to summon forth both saints and goddesses, while the vaguely Hindu communes in the west control lives. In its psychological and social attitudes, fundamentalism can include not only televangelists but some Roman Catholic enthusiasts, radical Muslims in Egypt (who hate Coptic Christians and unveiled women) or Stalinists in East Germany (who hate Chinese and Yugoslavian communist parties).

What Is Fundamentalism?

Fundamentalism offers simple answers to complex questions. Why are the questions complex? Because they are about God and us. For instance, Jesus is God, abortion is wrong, war is traditionally virtuous when aimed at God's enemies. The answers sound good! But Christianity patterned after the incarnation of the word of God in Jesus inquires further, looking at how both the human and the divine have their roles in Jesus, in the church and in us. Let us look again at these three topics: (1) Isn't Jesus also a human being, and is God not localized solely in Jesus of Nazareth? (2) Is the objectively evil act of abortion under awful circumstances for this particular woman always a sin? (3) Are wars which cripple or end civilization itself ever legitimate? These two-sided responses are not unorthodox but incarnational. In giving attention to both the human and the divine they are realistic and thought-provoking. They include needed distinctions so we can think like an adult and solve complicated issues. Often, Thomas Aquinas thought, like virtue and healthy life, truth lies in the middle.

But distinctions, thinking, complicated questions—aren't they just more relativism and uncontrolled liberalism? This two-sidedness, this ambiguity is precisely what fundamentalists fear.

Fundamentalism flourishes in a time of uncertainty because it offers instant and easy certainty. Fundamentalism indicates the manner in which many Americans now would like to think about their churches and faiths.

Let us begin by exploring some characteristics of Christian fundamentalism held in common by charismatics, evangelicals, every fundamentalist orientation. There is more to fundamentalisms than rapidly cited biblical passages. Our critique focuses on basic views concerning the nature of religion and God's presence outside of creation in what we call "grace," "revelation," or "the history of salvation." Watching on television a succession of preachers, movements and messages, the viewer can pick up a certain similarity. Let us look at three characteristics.

God in a Thing

A fundamentalist emphasizes the *location* of God's power and plan in some *thing*. For Protestant fundamentalists this is primarily the Bible. Christians believe the Bible is inspired, but for fundamentalists this inspiration of the Bible is total yet also superficial. Such inspiration appears simplistic, unrealistic and magical. The Bible is God's word, but it is also a collection of human writings. God does speak through them but precisely through their literary forms and their histories, sometimes in their poetry and stories. The poetry of an angel-guide for Tobiah or a home in a whale for Jonah is different from the narratives of the preaching and saving death of Jesus.

There are indeed general teachings and moral principles in the Bible (some of which are quite demanding) but we cannot, as Jimmy Swaggart does, derive foreign policy from the book of Genesis or solve new bio-medical issues from Romans.

In fundamentalism, the location of the divine lies ultimately not in the Bible's text but in the preacher, especially in the evangelist's personal theology. This evangelist's interpretation is special, unique in that it has no background or peer. In the last analysis God's word may be only a phrase ("Jesus as Lord and Savior"). The evangelist—man or woman, young or old—is the founder of the faith and church being preached and its sole leader. An open Bible is held, Jesus Christ is referred to intimately, "church" and "ministry" are presented, but this faith and church are ultimately those of the television preacher. The evangelist founded it, sustains and expands it, controls its employees and policies—in short, owns it. The norm of faith is this one interpretation of scripture.

Fundamentalism relies heavily on language, on religious language. The rights words are saving; the wrong words are offensive. Often the views of others are not presented fairly but are exaggerated through language which will frighten.

A Direct Line to God

A sacred thing, whether it be a Bible or a personal conversion, gives *easy* access to the divine. This automatic access not only lets me know what God wants but leads me to expect miraculous interventions at my beck and call. God tells the TV evangelists what to do: Oral Roberts' death, PTL's projects, and inevitably the solicitation of money.

Now a person with privileged links to God would be special. The New Testament says we (citizens and heirs of the kingdom of God) are special in God's eyes but not at the expense of other women and men. The kingdom is open to all; its boundaries are known only to God; its celebrities are its servants. For fundamentalisms, Christians (and they define just who they are) make up an elite which is not just humanly but divinely better than other people.

For the fundamentalist there are not levels of divine truth and of divine grace, not different ways of viewing God or of living out a Christian life. There is only one way. My preacher and I know it; thus we are better, even unique, in God's eyes. Those who do not have this special, identifiable way to God are not just underprivileged members of other Christian churches (or non-Christian religions) with their own traditions, but they are outside of God's love, message and grace. They must be lost. Why is fundamentalism so pugnacious, so ready for judgment and condemnation of others? Because its approach to religion and life needs to be instantly and easily right, so right that others are clearly wrong.

In fundamentalist movements there are no gray areas. Everything is clear. Russia's foreign policy is as certainly evil as Moses leading Israel out of Egypt was good. Charity toward a dying person is the same as not drinking a light beer; the Bible's accuracy is no different when it mentions Tobiah's dog than when it narrates the sermon on the mount; Romanian communists displease God as much as the money changers in the temple whom Jesus drove out.

To question, deny, or relegate to secondary significance any aspect of this preacher's message is to reject all of Christian revelation.

A God of Miracles

In fundamentalism, the divine power frequently intervenes in dramatic ways at the command of the elite (the leader of this church). God acts often in miracles, healings, voices, prophecies. Everything that happens to the evangelist, to his or her "ministry," is miraculous. Miracles are frequent in the divine world of fundamentalism. But miracles are rare in the New Testament, and Jesus praised those who lived by faith and love. On television, the prophet summons God to act miraculously. Moreover, the unique role of the evangelist as God's special representative in a fallen world is proven by miracles.

God is not a God of nature and creation, and particularly not a God of the unseen kingdom of God working really but invisibly in people; not a God of a sometimes desperate hope, or of the love which is kept modestly secret.

The fundamentalist ministry is further confirmed by what we might call "worldly miracles." There are to be successes in raising money, expanding transmitters and building structures. Money is important! Money shows which side God is on. Both checks and charisms are necessary to sustain publicly a ministry attracting the attention of audiences on earth . . . and in heaven.

The devil is prominent in fundamentalism, almost an evil deity, the shadow side of God. The devil too works in extraordinary ways. This diabolical show and activity, however, is often used as an excuse. When all else had failed, Jim and Tammy Faye Bakker stated that the devil had made Bakker dishonestly solicit money and engage in sexual libertinism. Deliberate sin, failures of society to pursue justice, the misery of those living in the subcultures of poverty in cities, sensuality and greed—all can be blamed on the devil. While sin often involves human weakness and emotional lack of control, significant and planned sin is not forced upon men and women by a fire-engulfed angel. Just as too much of the miraculous demeans the activity of God and people, so blaming the devil for consciously pursued evil turns people into puppets.

Defining Fundamentalism

Can we define this umbrella term "fundamentalism"? We are looking not at every creed or movement, at this or that church, but at a theological, social and psychological approach to Christianity. We are not defining rural southern Protestant Christianity but *Christian* fundamentalism wherever it is found. We are not ridiculing Christians and churches but evaluating a theological stance different from and even hostile to Catholicism. Christian fundamentalism is *an interpretation of Christianity in which a charismatic leader locates with easy certitude in chosen words, doctrines and practices the miraculous actions of a strict God saving an elite from an evil world.*

Ultimately, an argument with a fundamentalist comes down to how one sees reality. Can human life be trusted? Is creation good? Are people and politics usually sinful and dangerous?

A Different Perspective

Usually fundamentalism is defined in terms of literal adherence to the Bible, but this is only one facet of fundamentalism's full theology; miracles and healing, even buildings and clothes, can be as significant as the biblical page. The topic of these pages is not typical biblical fundamentalism, nor the variety and extent of fundamentalism. This is a look at the deeper Christian issues precisely as Catholicism differs from fundamentalism. James Barr observes that to look only at the biblical passages is almost to accept the fundamentalist point of view. There are other issues.

> Understanding what other forms of Christianity are like (is important). How is one to understand what "orthodoxy" means? How is one to understand how modern theologians actually think? How is one simply to get along with people whose religious views are vastly different from our own? In large measure fundamentalism is built not upon the Bible but upon its own peculiar picture of the outside world.[9]

Christian fundamentalism, of whatever sort, leads to the history of the church, the history of theology, relationship of creation to redemption and to the image and presence of God. "The defect of fundamentalism may be not, as its critics so often say, that its approach to Scripture is unhistorical, but rather that it is lacking in a sense for the total history of Christianity, from the Bible up to the present day."[10]

Eugene LaVerdiere observes that fundamentalism flourishes among those who amid a constantly changing society can find no stable position in society, or who in depressed economic conditions are without prospects for the future. We cannot overlook the fact that these *do* need divine assistance.

> It should not surprise us to find fundamentalists in populations of poor immigrants for whom church structures in the land to which they have immigrated are inadequate. Nor should it amaze us to find it among those who find themselves suddenly out of work and who watch their savings erode daily. We should also expect to find it among students who struggle with their studies and who know that even if they succeed they may not find a place for themselves in the world of work. Should we wonder that such people see the world around them as coming to an end? Even among the wealthy and middle class, fundamentalism can provide a buttress against changes which threaten their way of life, privilege, and status.[11]

Fundamentalism also flourishes among middle class adults fed by their anxiety over change and reluctance to think. The convinced, psychologically fixated fundamentalist can ruin a family, wreck a parish, harm a university program. Human beings have always found an array of things ready to be identified with God— sacred pages, translations of religious texts, phrases in foreign languages, gestures and clothes, geographical places and buildings— and other innocent creations identified with the demonic—food, drink, dancing, playing cards, plays, clothes, machines, buttons, musical instruments, skin color. As we will see, the preaching of

Jesus removes any magic from the ordinary things of life as he offers not divisions to the human race but maturity and community in God's realm.

The following is a "Catholic perspective" on fundamentalism: it criticizes the characteristics of every fundamentalism from basic principles of the Catholic understanding of Christian life and community. This book presents a particular perspective or understanding of Christianity. Part One sketches the vitality and diversity of fundamentalism, mainly in its Protestant forms, but also in movements which touch the Roman Catholic Church more directly. Part Two offers psychology and theology and central ideas which illustrate the differences between the essence of Catholicism (which is not always found in every shrine and every political theologian) and the essence of fundamentalism (which is not the same as respect for the historical narratives of the Bible). Theological critique and perspective eventually reach the incarnation, the presence of God's word in an individual human being. Between personal, devotional infallibility and relative, agnostic secularity lies a middle ground of complexity where divine personal love and human individuality mix. This is the school of the incarnation, the realm of the kingdom of God.

2

Catholic Fundamentalisms

"Uncreated first truth is one. But from it, however, many truths exist in created minds, likenesses of that first truth."
THOMAS AQUINAS

Fundamentalism is a worldwide movement and a psychological stance. Can we speak of fundamentalism within Roman Catholicism? Catholics do not usually cite biblical passages with fire in their eyes; indeed, one can still hear about Irish or Bohemian parents who considered reading the Bible to be "Protestant." Does a Catholic fundamentalism exist? Wouldn't fundamentalism exclude Catholic features? Fundamentalism, however, can exist in politics or religion, in personal life or in science. Anything can become "fundamentalized."

A "Catholic" Fundamentalism?

Fundamentalism can appear in any church, in any religion, in any political party. Television transmits the pictures of fundamentalist Muslim clergy from Iran to Libya. There can be fundamentalist devotees of baroque music who disdain Tchaikovsky, fundamentalist Leninists who reject any move to independent farms and shops, and fundamentalist Republicans who oppose all federal assistance.

Every fundamentalism has a similar psychology. One of the curious developments of the past decade is the cooperation between far right and the far left, although, if able, they would outlaw each other. Far right-wing Republicans agree with socialist-minded Democrats that ordinary liberalism should be stopped. Catholic sectarians who erroneously think that the Catholic Church should barely tolerate Protestants work together with televangelists who consider Rome to be the whore of Babylon. A rigid and total fundamentalist stance seems to be more important than the needs and opportunities of people's lives. So with fundamentalism as a psychological stance able to enter most movements, it is not surprising that there are fundamentalists within the Catholic Church.

The Jesuit sociologist John Coleman argues that Catholic "integrism," the claim to be the true church while the church of Vatican II sold out to modernity, is a major danger. He notes that both Protestant and Catholic fundamentalisms began at the beginning of this century; both wish to enjoy the technological benefits of the modern world while claiming to live in a religious community apart from modernity. For Catholics, a "creeping infallibility" of the papacy accomplishes what the biblical page does for Protestants. "Catholic integralists are very vocal in denying that any such thing as papal fundamentalism exists. They claim that the only form of fundamentalism is (Protestant) biblical fundamentalism. . . . The virtue of studying the variety of fundamentalisms in the world religions is that it reminds us that each has its own homegrown variety."[1]

Catholic fundamentalism? What would that be?

We are not discussing Catholics who have become Protestant fundamentalists but the psychological and religious forms within Roman Catholicism.

What would fashion a Catholic fundamentalism? We are not speaking of Catholics with conservative tendencies; today one can have legitimate preferences in liturgy or politics. It would be hard to describe monastic orders like the Trappists, Benedictines, and Discalced Carmelites as anything but conservative. In a sense, the Catholic Church remains by its very tradition and nature generally conservative. Patrick Arnold writes: "Protestant fundamentalism's growing attractiveness is rightly regarded by Catholic officials as a threat to the integrity of their communities in the United States and Latin America. Less well recognized, however, is the fact that the Catholic community in the United States is even more severely threatened by the rise of its own distinctive brand of fundamentalism."[2]

Today there is a parade of Catholic fundamentalisms. Someone who knows little about the structure and history of the Vatican curia complains when any discourse of the pope is criticized. Born-again businessmen may be dubious about the salvation of their fellow Catholics. New, unapproved religious orders of men and women attract novices by stating that Jesuits and Franciscans are no longer faithful to their traditions. A few parishes with recent miracles decide to be God's voice to the world. There is also a fundamentalism of the immediate past where young reactionaries seek to restore some form of neo-scholastic thought or vestments no longer used. What they imagine to be medieval or baroque (times of pluralism and creativity) are, in fact, recent forms born of the past century.

Fundamentalism always places great power in words. Recently Catholic fundamentalists have begun to redefine and control the word "orthodoxy." Orthodoxy means not the writings of Ambrose or Bonaventure but the piety of this group. Just as Protestant fundamentalists are attempting to make "Christian" mean a follower of a televangelist, so Catholic fundamentalists use "orthodox" to mean someone who thinks as they do.

Fundamentalism always lies close to what the group feels is most important. Certain Protestant churches founded between 1830 and 1980 turned the personal experience of justification and the biblical page into sacred things that bless pre-selected people in a sinful world. It is easy to see how the Bible becomes a religious object; a book, the Bible, could give answers and rules. Justification is a person's relationship to God's presence, invisible, hidden in the depth of human psyche. But "born again," "baptized in the spirit," "accepting the Lord," are religious phrases describing not so much the mystery of my life with God but a sinner upon which an external, miraculous shaft of approval has fallen. (Luther would have been horrified at easy and miraculous justification!)

Catholic fundamentalists will possess a certain rigid and narrow attention to some object or practice. "Though its American adherents like to refer to their movement as 'neo-orthodoxy' or 'reform,' the term 'Catholic fundamentalism' probably best suits this ideology since the phrase not only invites comparison with comparable movements in other world religions, but also permits the distinctively Catholic qualities of the movement to emerge."[3]

At the Heart of the Matter

Catholics are ill at ease with Bible shoot-outs. Nor do they rejoice in suddenly finding out in their adult life that they are "saved," or that they should be born again. The fundamentalist mind will select and exaggerate something central, something at the heart of the religious movement. For Protestants, it might be the Bible or baptism in the Holy Spirit, while Muslims fight over the black rock at Mecca, and Marxists argue over the text of Lenin.

The essence of Catholicism, as we will see in Chapter 5, is the sacramental. "Sacramental" here does not mean the eucharist or baptism. At the depth of the sacramental lies the presence and mediation, the interplay of God's grace and creation's world and people. Catholics, it is not surprising, will find their fundamentalism in (1) sacramental things and in (2) church authority.

Sacramental things and activities are places where God's grace can be present, can be seen and heard. Protestants and secular non-believers have traditionally been put off by the "things" of Catholicism: the statues with their symbolic roses or arrows, the incense smoke or the candle's fire, the eucharistic bread and wine of such a real presence that it should be publicly so acknowledged, or people with real authority in the church. Human beings, however, love pictures and dramas. The portrayal of the divine in human life is inevitable. People want to see and touch the incarnations of grace. Those churches which have eliminated in the name of "purity" the visual and the liturgical have rarely found large followings beyond one country, one class and one era.

Protestantism, however, should legitimately object to things which claim to enclose or manipulate grace, for the Protestant suspicion of idolatry and superstition in things is rooted in Jesus' preaching, rejecting the localization or control of grace. As long as it is a respected presence and not a magic performance, the sacramental continues the union of the human and the divine in Jesus. Catholicism in its essential commitment to the sacramental is not fundamentalism. There can be people and ceremonies, materials and colors which—without claiming to manipulate grace—make present and visualize God's presence.

Blessed Things and Holy Figures

Fundamentalism enters Roman Catholicism when it invests the created—a statue, a medal, a ritual—with an exaggerated divine power. It is not the reality of divine grace or the sacramental inter-play of the created and the divine which is objectionable but the localization and manipulation of a personal, divine presence, of God's free love. The easy production and control by human beings of what is God's power is magic. Catholic fundamentalism has two main forms: the first locates divine power in created things like a medal or a statue; the second locates divine revelations in author-ities. Let us look briefly at each.

God in Material Things

Catholic church-goers in Sicily and New York, farmers and bishops in Ireland or Austria, can fall into a fundamentalism of things. Emphasizing to an extreme the divine presence and action in something created is a fundamentalism. Demanding the saint's plaster statue to dispense miracles is magic. Miracles are rare in the kingdom of ordinary grace, medals will not always protect from human disasters, and one religious ritual will not guarantee an eternal salvation. The devotee can act as if the statue *is* the dead but heavenly person, as if the plaster and wood are the shell for an unstoppable power waiting to be tapped. The statue can become a minor deity who must be not just petitioned but wheedled, cajoled, even bribed by dollars to influence God, or to alter the course of life.

Saints are important to Catholics because of their individual, Christian lives. These men and women lived a mixture of suffering and joy, good and evil, and their statues remind us of their exem-plary lives, vivid but past. They have gone before us, are members of the wider Christian family and are interested in our lives, but they are not sorcerers. Christianity is not "insider-trading" with angels and saints, or with God. The beauties of art in paintings and statues tell us the biblical message for our own lives. We are not called to be a clone of St. Francis or St. Thérèse, but, aided by God's grace and loved by the prayers of such saints, we are destined to be the unique saint which is our own destiny. So prayer and liturgy, sacramentals and medals, exist not to control the divine being but to make concrete the hidden presence of God in our special individuality.

God in Authorities

Organization and institution come to mind with the words "Roman Catholic Church." The Vatican is not just a site for museums but a cluster of organizational apparatuses administering a worldwide church. Moreover, this church recognizes in its central administration a doctrinal and moral authority binding upon all its members.

To belong to the Catholic Church is to remain freely within an organization which accepts past doctrinal statements about God, humanity and Christ. There is too a basic ethics and a continuing intent to evaluate new moral issues, medical, sexual and political. Canon law governs the legal and administrative processes of the church, while liturgical rubrics guide church services.

All of these structures of authority fade into the background, however, when that figure emerges who dominates the panorama of authority in the Roman Catholic Church: the pope. The infallible pope—this is a forceful authority. The fundamentalism of authority is the particularly forceful form of Catholic fundamentalism today. What an enthusiastically literal, if selective, reading of the Bible is to Protestant fundamentalism, the appeal to a few Vatican documents or to imaginary or imprecise papal stances, an appeal to an abstract and distant authority, is dominant Catholic fundamentalism.

Pondering such credentials, we may ask: Is not every religious authority in the Catholic Church of the same style, infallible? Can there be a critique of authority in the Catholic Church?

Human beings and communities need authority. We make progress through the authority of parents, teachers, coaches, priests, presidents. Authority can bring us a state of peace, ease the tensions of ignorance and failure. If humans at times rebel against authority, ultimately they must also embrace authority, for they cannot live in anarchy. As history shows, authority can become exaggerated, frozen, injurious, even demonic; at this point it is no longer "authority" but "authoritarianism," or even "totalitarianism." Authority can imprison or anesthetize. After the French Revolution there came an authority more violent than liberating; after the modern world wars there arose Hitler and Stalin. Even as human beings revolt to search for their own peace and freedom, they want authority.

The search for authority (or for one specific authority) lies at the heart of every fundamentalism. Every fundamentalism is an espousal of some authority with an embrace which is stifling.

In the Catholic Church authority can become for some members a fundamentalism. First, authority in the central revelation of God to us through Christ is one thing, while asserting easy authority in changing social and political matters is something else. Second, although one church leader in rare moments has a special guidance (expressed in the inept English word "infallible"), such an intense inspiration is not present daily, or in every church leader. Third, there can be a presumption that exercise of church authority requires no preparation: no study, no ability, no consultation. All three of these abuses of the authority of bishops and popes exist. Individuals, albeit of a lofty church office, do not expand or manipulate but serve God's word. In authority, too, God acts less in extraordinary displays than in ordinary ways.

Saying that Catholics can view church authority in a fundamentalist manner is not a rejection of the levels of authority in church leaders. Fundamentalism in authority arises as an easy remedy for anxiety amid change; some miraculous power out there makes it no longer necessary for my conscience to make decisions, or for theologians to consider new scientific issues.

Catholic Fundamentalists

We have just listed ways in which today a fundamentalist attitude can take hold of some Roman Catholics. Fundamentalism aims consciously or unconsciously at the solo: only these words should be employed; only this church group is salvific. The movement of Archbishop Lefebvre, who recently went into schism from Rome, can be one illustration here. Lefebvre's followers make up a very small but worldwide movement (centered largely in France) which is not just conserving a liturgy from the sixteenth century but is formally rejecting the teachings of the ecumenical council, Vatican II, in favor of previous pieties and theologies.

> Traditionalist Catholics are not a "fringe" element of antiquarian malcontents as much as a "hard" expression of diffuse estrangement on the Catholic right consequent upon the tensions and strain generated by Vatican II's change and reform. What Archbishop Lefebvre has done is to transform this estrangement—through the rhetoric of subversion, conspiracy, heresy, injustice and eschatological urgency (and with episcopal authority)—into a counter-church movement opposing those who have "infected" Catholicism from within with the "viruses" of liberalism and modernism.[4]

Lefebvre is not asking for modifications in some documents of Vatican II but rejects the entire event as a capitulation to communism and secularity. He verges on heresy in his views concerning the extent of grace to women and men who are not Catholics. Extolling baroque monarchies and the counter-reformation, he sees the Vatican as capitulating to the Protestant reformation and the French (and American) Revolution from which have come all the evils of modernity. "At Vatican II, according to the Archbishop, the 'false principles' of Protestantism, liberalism and modernism unleashed by these 'revolutions' were assimilated into the church. . . . Lefebvre's response has been to try to convince Catholics that the proximate cause of the crisis is more than a wrong interpretation of the council but flows from the council itself."[5]

Vatican II was a decisive break with the church's past, hence with its tradition, and so not only heresy and schism but a "new church" are emerging. "The point should not be missed that Lefebvre's attack on the council was well underway before the emergence of any alleged 'abuses' of its reforms. Furthermore, the Archbishop's separatist actions for nearly two decades also speak reams about his willingness 'to accept' the council. In light of these initiatives, one can only suspect whistling in the dark when it is asserted that the traditionalist movement consists of Catholics whose principle [sic] grievance is no more than the 'incorrect applications' of

Vatican II reforms."[6] Catholic traditionalism, like Protestant fundamentalism, does not appear as a group slightly irritated by a new social or theological viewpoint; it fears a contemporary world and seeks to preserve a religious experience which is antiquarian.

Catholic fundamentalism is of a special sort. Fundamentalist Catholics are even more cerebral than Protestant ones; the Bible is made up of narratives and parables, while Catholics canonize Aristotelian axioms and Latin phrases. Nevertheless, large numbers of men and women today, middle-aged New Englanders or young Californians, are not going to have their interest held by theological nuggets from neo-scholastic textbooks. So the focus of Catholic fundamentalists has been, since Vatican II, the liturgy. They are entranced by the Tridentine rite (the "Latin mass"), although other rites of east and west existed before and after its birth in the sixteenth century. A second focus is politics, for it is felt that popes, bishops and theologians have become too concerned about poverty and injustice.

Lefebvre and his followers represent both political and liturgical fundamentalisms. They have focused upon the rubrics and Latin language of the Tridentine mass, preferring baroque and nineteenth century rites to the patristic and the medieval, and arguing that the present liturgy (partly dating from the third century) does not incarnate the eucharistic theology of the Council of Trent. They have also engaged in a battle over where church authority lies, preferring interestingly a past piety to the authority of popes and an ecumenical council. There are also the elements of the apocalyptic (Vatican II is a "revolution," "capitulation" or "schism") and of hatred of the world (Protestants, Buddhists, etc. are not viewed favorably). The recent failure of the Vatican's strained policy of reconciliation shows that "sectarianism has no vocabulary of compromise, nor can sectarian movements be quietly co-opted into existing ecclesial structures."[7]

The Lefebvre movement is a clear if radical form of Catholic fundamentalism preferring an imaginary papal authority to the real one, devoted to sacral objects rather than to Christian lives. Other less publicized and less separatist groups are numerous. There are "sedevacantists" (from the Latin for the see of Rome being vacant after the death of a pope) who hold that no legitimate pope has functioned since John XXIII and that all liturgical acts since Vatican II are invalid. *Opus Dei* is an organization for laity (only males have full membership) with much secrecy and sustained by a thin, immature spirituality (quite inferior to the great schools of the spiritual life) and an avoidance of theology. Its founder Josemaria Scriva di Balanguer wrote in 1972 that the post-conciliar era was filled with rottenness and sin, corruptions emanating from within church leadership and from high up.[8] Members of *Opus Dei* have recently accused the American bishops of being permissive in matters of sexuality, and more interested in politics than piety. What characterizes groups and individuals pointing to collapse in the Catholic Church (in fact, in the world and in the United States the Catholic Church has reached a remarkable stage of practice and growth) is an utter ignorance about history, an idealization of the anemic age of the 1950s, and a lack of interest concerning both theology and daily life. Pope John Paul in his letter urging Archbishop Lefebvre to be reconciled to the church wrote that a Catholic may not prefer the past to its present and that tradition does not exclude development. "By tradition, the Church remains, through the changing circumstances of history, faithful to the truth received."[9]

There are also Catholic fundamentalisms of the exaggerated left, theologies and politics which have their own jargon and causes. There too people are excluded for a lack of rigidity in radicalism, for differing perspectives on how to change the world. Every good cause, for instance serving the poor or working for peace, can become a fundamentalism. Then it views every lack of immediate success as satanic and other political visions as fallen. Liberal fundamentalism in social action and church renewal comes easily, since the rate of change is slow for a church which is catholic, for an entire nation, for a world.

Catholic Fundamentalism: A Preliminary Critique

This book's sketch of the Catholic perspective differing from fundamentalism is found mainly in Chapters 5 and 6. But there are general observations along this line in every chapter. Here we offer, in an anticipatory way, a critique by Catholic theology of the fundamentalist deformation of Catholicism.

Catholics must be very clear about what constitutes an idol. The Christian cannot exchange the Spirit of God for stones, for Latin or for a recent vision. Catholics should not confuse the sacramental (which in liturgy and papacy is rejected by Protestant fundamentalists) with the magical, which is control over God.

Church authority is intended to deal with life in the centuries, the millennia which follow Jesus. Catholicism claims that the authority of the Christian faith is not something purely of the past, nor is it found solely in ancient books. Church authority for Catholics is not just the decisions of bishops acting as company officials, nor is it divine voices dictating easy rules and decisions. The human and the divine are both at work. The roles of the community's leaders— bishops and pope—are explicit and central. But there are also roles for others in the church—for theologians, charismatics, various ministers, and others among the baptized. Neither a democracy nor a monarchy, the Catholic Church arranges in patterns the players who contribute to decision-making in the church. These models have different emphases from one historical period to another. The pope coordinates, leads, evaluates and participates in the process of the worldwide community but he does not assume all the roles in the church.

Protestant fundamentalism appeals to the authority of the Bible (and indirectly to the charism of the evangelist), while Catholic fundamentalism appeals to the authority of the pope. To be a Catholic is to believe that the Holy Spirit remains with the church, protecting the revelation of Christ. Out of that infallibility of the church comes the special roles of the bishops as leaders and of the bishop of Rome as leader of the bishops. What is challenged today by the burst of new bio-medical and social issues, by the education of people and by the presentations of the media is an uncritical and untheological, a pious, almost mythical view that the pope alone plays every role in decision-making in the church; and, secondly, that every statement by anyone in the Vatican is incapable of change or error. This fundamentalism is consoling for those who identify grace with a catechism of ideas and who wish to be consoled (some in a self-sufficient secularity) by the assurance that somewhere there is a magical person who is an answering-machine. Walter Kasper writes of the new pluralism of theologies (not of faiths or dogmatic cores!) in the worldwide church after Vatican II.

> The question is how the church's unity in faith can still be made visible in these circumstances. Hasn't this process already made the church's testimony unclear? Hasn't it lost its unequivocalness and clarity? This is a worrying question. One answer, however, is ruled out, and that is a return to a position based solely on official authority. Not only is this theologically indefensible because it contradicts the truth that all have a mission and a responsibility, but it could also not be successful, at least not in the long run. . . . Once questions have emerged, it may be possible to suppress them temporarily, but they will not go away for good. This means that any conservative or traditionalist movement must also argue its case, and all argument inevitably provokes new questions.[10]

For Kasper authority serves the scriptures and the dogmas and ecumenical councils serve the church. To reject central beliefs is certainly unacceptable and a disintegration into an individualistic, liberal pluralism avoids the authority of Jesus the risen Christ and his Spirit, past and present, precisely as they work in the body of Christ, the ministering church. But in terms of today's new problems he advocates "orthodoxy through dialogue." Not all groups and members of the church have the same office, but many—theologians, bishops, laity, experts—have the right to a listening and contribution out of their expertise.

This mode of authority in an age of widespread education and international media networks is not so foreign to the process of authority in the Catholic Church which for centuries existed within a complex, multi-layered process. The pope and bishops exist within circles of other limited authorities, whether they be theologians or charismatic figures. The Vatican issues different kinds of documents with different degrees of binding authority. Qualifications indicating dogma and infallibility are carefully noted in church documents and apply to few statements. And today the contributions of the church in all areas of the world, of experts in science and sociology, of the churches made up of all the baptized as well as of bishops and theologians, further the dialogue which aims at hearing and orthodoxy.

Kasper concludes with an idea from the great theologian J.A. Möhler which is pertinent for a critique of fundamentalism. There are two extremes in the life of the church and both are forms of egoism: in the first everyone wants to be everything; in the second one person wants to be everything.

The fundamentalist imagines and speaks of hierarchy and magisterium as a distant machine set off from life and learning. It is not regard for the truth of revelation and the pastoral service of grace which sustains the compulsion that all church authority is infallible, but a personal need to locate and use this authority. Interestingly, Catholic fundamentalists can go so far as to reject church authority fully—in the name of their individual authority ("more Catholic than the pope"). Reactionary groups of laity or splinter religious congregations reject not just a Vatican decree or a papal encyclical, but pope and council. This is the negative side of an all-or-nothing attitude toward church authority. Either every piece of paper issued by the Vatican is infallible, or Catholic church authority is weak and erroneous.

Fundamentalism is a psycho-social mode of dealing with the modern world. Catholic fundamentalists have some characteristics in common with the followers of the televangelist, old and new. Sometimes they are drawn to his politics and world-denouncing rhetoric even though he himself sees Catholicism, along with Islam and communism, as the three enemies of Christ.

While fundamentalism can quite properly be linked with a zealous brand of conservative evangelical Protestantism, the term is now generally understood to denote a generic religious response to modernity. Protestant fundamentalism has been associated with a dogmatic, paranoid, dichotomous, literal and exclusivistic cognitive style, with right-wing political orientations, with a "church against the world" ecclesiology and with a belligerent proclivity to do battle against all partisans of error. All of these elements are evident within the Catholic traditionalist movement. Furthermore, traditionalism also manifests the classic fundamentalist tendency to absolutize the cognitive aspects of religion and to reify the constituent symbols of religious identity.[11]

Like the televangelists, Catholic fundamentalists have in fact founded their own church. They decide what they will accept from an authority they have insisted is always infallible. Interested more in recent visions than in new movements in Latin America, they substitute grandfather's devotions for liturgical renewal rooted in the third century.

A fundamentalist personality or *politique* can unite Catholic fundamentalists with Protestants over a particular issue: both are anxious about change and relativism. What emerges from the fundamentalist mind as it touches authority is nervous concern over other people's freedom. Will not people left free vote wrongly, turn to sin, leave the church, ignore the gospel? This is an un-Catholic, excessively Augustinian, discouragement about human nature left to itself. Since God's grace is present unceasingly to all, why should we fear freedom; why should we not rather work to enhance God's work by enhancing human initiative—a stance suggested by the theological shift at Vatican II?

At the level of politics, Catholic fundamentalism becomes sectarian. It opposes the harmony of nature and grace in Aquinas, and becomes hostile toward the cultures and governments of people. Rejecting any appeal to society (for society like human nature is sunk in original sin) and blind to the patterns of slow history, it inevitably ends in sectarianism. There, amid small groups of the perfect, having accomplished very little, it can nourish the shrine of its hidden dogma or purity. Hence sectarians within and without the Catholic Church are hostile toward the traditional approach of bishops and popes to social questions. In that approach, the realms of the human as well as the gospel have their contribution; and no strict separation is made between a perfect church and a sinful world, but the church, as sign, sacrament, liturgy and realization of the kingdom of God, invites all touched by grace (and invites members of the church to a more critical and deeper life and service of grace) to labor in history for God's own future.

Political fundamentalist coalitions, however, are not really an option for Catholics. Catholic fundamentalists are often uncommitted to the social teaching of the church, while Protestant fundamentalists, as the American bishops pointed out, reject many facets of Catholic faith, e.g. church and sacraments.

What troubles Catholic fundamentalists is history! The Catholic Church is living history. The different religious orders—Benedictines, Franciscans, Maryknoll—are signs of pluralism. Great saints (whose statues adorn the church) disagreed over theology and spirituality. The middle ages was a time of great Christian reflection, but scholasticism existed in schools which disagreed with each other over serious theological issues without confusing their views with dogma.

As C.S. Lewis observed: what we consider to be ancient is usually the product of the cultural period just before our own. What Catholic fundamentalists view as old and venerable, what excites them in a world of dim sacristies and short liturgies, has little to do with most of the Catholic Church's history. The past in the imagination of Catholic fundamentalists is largely a product of the nineteenth century and the baroque (this recalls G.K. Chesterton's observation that the neo-gothic nineteenth century "saw the middle ages by moonlight"). What Vatican II altered was not the church of the fathers and the middle ages—even the medieval orders like the Trappists and Dominicans had their religious life modified by church authority in terms of the nineteenth century. The liturgy and theology of today have a stronger claim to antiquity than the fiddle-back vestments and the textbooks of the 1890s.

So the Catholic fundamentalist is anti-traditional and anti-sacramental. He fears western Catholicism as Christianity-in-history. But tradition and grace are the energies by which human beings under the Spirit have through the centuries brought their culture and personality to Christian faith and church.

3

A False Ecumenism

"The one indispensable answer to an environment bristling with people and things one thought were bad was to go on finding out new ways in which one could think they were bad."

KINGSLEY AMIS,
"LUCKY JIM"

The twentieth century brought to the Christian churches—Protestant, Orthodox and Roman Catholic—the blessings of ecumenism, i.e. the movement toward Christian unity. Ecumenism has created positive relationships among Christian churches. Churches who have different traditions of Christian life and different ways of worship have ceased attacking each other and have recognized how each church proclaims much of God's revelation in Christ. For Catholics and Protestants in the United States the ecumenical movement in the 1960s quickly replaced past attitudes of bitter prejudice and mutual condemnation. Christians have learned to live together not just in tolerance but in mutual appreciation, acknowledging the depths of truth and grace which unite them.

A "New Ecumenism" and Fundamentalism

Unfortunately there has emerged in the 1980s a "new ecumenism"; it is, in fact, a false ecumenism, because it divides Protestants from Catholics, and unites Catholics and Protestants for dubious, wrong reasons. This false ecumenism is fundamentalist in its theology and sectarian in its view of the church in the world. It does not so much proselytize Catholics for membership in other churches but aims at convincing Catholics that their church is unorthodox, unfaithful to Christian history, in danger of succumbing to secularism.

False ecumenism brings together Catholic and Protestant extremists. Such a relationship would not normally exist, for the ideologies of each exclude the conviction that any other group could see the truth. But they are united by their dislike of the middle ground which they despise, often inaccurately, as relativistic liberalism. Catholics, even some clergy, are ignorant of the essential characteristics of Catholicism; they confuse them with externals, memories of youth, a parish established for immigrants. A few of these externals of the nineteenth century (this blessed medal, that novena) faded away after Vatican II while the forms of others became renewed in Catholic life. Most aspects of Roman Catholicism remained through the great upheaval after Vatican II; there has been relatively little challenge to the great dogmas of Christianity.

Still, a few changes in externals can make some fearful of change itself. The fundamentalist mind can confuse change in forms with change in substance—fearing, for instance, that a liturgy in English has altered faith in the eucharist, or that any criticism of church authority is rejection of papal and conciliar infallibility. Consequently, some Catholics abandon the synthesis, so characteristic of Thomas Aquinas, of faith and pastoral application, of grace and personality, and they choose a nostalgia of things or the emotion of world-hating. This sectarian stance is quite different from the historical life of Catholicism with its eight hundred million members and various traditions ranging from Greek to Indian cultures. What is tragic in this unecumenical union of disgruntled Catholics with fundamentalists—evangelists and scholars, theologians and politicians are involved—is the abandonment of the living center of Catholicism for a dualistic sectarianism, and the surrender of the middle ground where grace meets human life created good and redeemed.

We are interested in this negative "ecumenism." It is a movement directed at the contemporary life of Roman Catholicism, where a variety of fundamentalists are at work today to *reform* Catholicism. Not knowing the history of Catholicism or experiencing its life, the "new ecumenists," nevertheless, want to alter the Catholic Church, to impose upon the worldwide church their ideas of what Catholicism ought to be. What is most important is that all

reject the Catholic Church *as it has existed in history and as it
is today.*

A false ecumenism does not offer the insights of Calvin and
Luther, of Tillich and Barth to Catholics. These are gifts of Christians whose traditions offer helpful and profound approaches to the
gospel. Rather, this reform movement directed at the Roman
Catholic Church is born of fundamentalist fears. This false dialogue
embraces neither the Protestant principle nor the Catholic substance. If one looks closely, one sees a reformist voicing of pre-ecu-
menical complaints about the church cloaked by a ceaseless critique
of society.

Reforming the Catholic Church

This false ecumenism is a *fundamentalist reformism disdainful
of the Catholic vision.* Ranging from university campuses to television programs a variety of figures and movements express a reactionary criticism of the Catholic Church today and they wish to
reform it. It is anti-Catholic in its heritage, theology and goals.

The decline of the antiquarian dimension of liturgy is regretted
by some. Is a variety of liturgical celebrations—for a solemn assem-
bly, for children, for the sick of a parish—a capitulation to secularism? For others political factors are more important. The moves of
the Catholic Church in the sphere of politics—liberation theology
in Latin America, the socialist concerns of a Polish pope, the American bishops' letters on war and the economy—produce agitation.
Is the Roman Catholic Church moving too far to the left? Does it
need their correction?

Some supporters of this false ecumenism are neo-conservative
political theorists who would save the Catholic Church from mixing
in the world's affairs. They find in the church's public discussion of
difficult ethical issues like war and poverty the liberalism they fear.
They argue that the church has become uncertain and indecisive,
because it recognizes that authority should include deliberation and
consultations, and that social change (demanded by Jesus' preaching) is slow. They would welcome papal authority—but for the right
causes. One finds Protestants here intoxicated with the idea that
they might become mentors of the Catholic Church today. Fright-

ened by the picture of Catholics criticizing the pope or making retreats at Buddhist monasteries, they see their mission to convince Catholics to embrace the theology (if not the church) of sectarian Protestantism. A third group are antiquarians fascinated by the ritual and organization of the Catholic Church. Although they may not share a Catholic's belief in the eucharistic presence and are exempt from obedience to the bishop of Rome, they find baroque church rituals like the use of incense to be more important than the church's presence in western politics or Asian societies. The experience of priests and sisters who have spent forty years in schools, hospitals or missions are dismissed by these outsiders because these Catholics lack interest in the bishop's bugia. Anxiety before modernity fuels this false ecumenism, a sectarian rigidity which can run roughshod over the essence of Catholicism.

The View from the Outside

Concerned with externals but not raised in a sacramental community, outsiders may see changes in devotional phrases or in liturgical gestures as significant. They can easily approach Catholicism as a museum, or identify the faith of millions with an Irish catechism or a past pope. The museum is a place where aesthetic and mystical forms are still found and there one is only a tourist— an outsider—among religious beauty. (This museum, of course, existed in a few monasteries, but does not generally do justice to the boring insouciance of the average parish's life before Vatican II.) Gregorian chant (imagined to have had an existence beyond a few minutes at Christmas mass) and Latin seminary textbooks (which barely conceded grace to any Protestant) are symbols of a golden age. The authority of the pope is longed for, but desired to preserve the antiquarian and the trivial in Christianity, not to address the new challenges of the contemporary world.

The outsider can afford to encourage strict authority because there is no threat that the professional or spiritual life of a non-Catholic will be intruded upon. The outside critic will never be touched by this authority.

Ecumenical Protestants who come to know the Roman Catholic Church a little from the inside are surprised by it. They expect an authority-ridden monolith but find an array of many groups. The power and variety of the religious orders (most older than American Protestant fundamentalism, and not a few founded centuries before Luther or Columbus), the struggle of old and new institutions to live and minister, contribute diversity. Catholicism, in fact, has a lengthy experience of variety in forms. Although it may defend (vigorously for a while) the status quo, deep down it knows that the grace and life of Christianity and Catholicism come through forms given by the arts and philosophies of cultures living in history. In terms of authority, the basic beliefs of Christianity cannot be rejected, and there are always current issues about which the Vatican feels strongly; apart from these there is considerable freedom in this church.

Saving and Teaching the Catholic Church

Among those intent upon saving the Catholic Church are recent converts. Although quite vocal, some (not all!) have a shallow or skewed understanding of Catholicism. Converts can be antiquarians or seekers after security. Unfortunately, they can become hostile to those raised in the Catholic Church, finding them too relaxed, too liberal in the Catholic sacramental world. They like a Catholicism of the past: a quiet chapel with street noises kept out.

Curiously, in the process of conversion these individuals did not change, did not move from one tradition to another. They have entered not the Catholic Church as it exists; they have entered a set of pictures or an idea in their mind. This type of convert does not pursue a process of "becoming" a Catholic but sets out immediately to "reform" the church they just entered. They are always seeking for a church to be their private church.

Some fundamentalists—scholars and teachers as well as evangelists of the campus or the airwaves—fear that Catholicism will not be able to meet modernity and at the same time represent orthodox Christianity (although in the past thirty years that union has perdured). Centers of Catholic life attract the new fundamentalist reformers. Zeal draws them to church institutions where they can denounce or instruct. The University of Notre Dame (where I have taught for a decade) is a national center of American Catholicism.

Perhaps that explains why it has become a crossroads, sometimes a battleground, of individuals and groups intent upon reforming the Roman Catholic Church—from the outside.

The following figures have crossed my path in the past two years alone.

- A young southern graduate student in philosophy, after only a few months of contact with Roman Catholics, complained emotionally that the general of the Jesuits in Rome was too permissive toward Jesuit moral theologians.
- An ethician wondered why the American Catholic bishops, after issuing their letter on nuclear war, did not simply command all Catholics to obey the letter of this document (he did not say whether under pain of sin or just excommunication).
- A sectarian theoretician on church and society was indignant at a papal encyclical's "exegetical simplicities" and its gestures toward non-Christians and urged (in Indiana!) an end to all papal encyclicals.
- A historian from a fundamentalist college lectured that Catholicism owned only two theologies: before and after Vatican II. The second was based upon an unfortunate and uncritical acceptance of history and subjectivism contrary to the absoluteness of the gospel. The speaker was surprised to hear of the variety of theological approaches (developed by religious orders) within Roman Catholicism during the medieval and baroque periods.
- A missionary (with his family) from a small, independent Baptist group came to evangelize the Notre Dame undergraduates. A letter-winner in college, he described in his church paper how he had used sports to make contact with athletes; then dinners would lead to studying the Bible. His report indicated that he viewed the students' Catholicism as an unfortunate religion unrelated to Christ.
- A candidate for a junior position in theology (he was from a Protestant sectarian background and was finishing a doctorate in religious studies at a large university) gave a lecture on how the "superficial" and "liberal" Karl Rahner needed to be corrected by Thomas Aquinas. Few of his teachers were acquainted with modern or medieval Catholic theology, and the candidate was

unaware that Rahner had in some ways restored Aquinas' thought in this area to prominence.

■ The student daily newspaper periodically contains long essays complaining that Notre Dame students have lost their faith because they question some papal views on sex and family life; about half the articles are written by Protestant fundamentalists or recent converts.

Catholic campuses become a place of multiple evangelization. *Our Sunday Visitor* did a series of articles describing how well-funded fundamentalist groups operate on many Catholic campuses. They listed: Campus Crusade, The Navigators, Inter-Varsity Christian Fellowship and University Bible Fellowship. Although such groups will vigorously assert they are non-denominational (which is not incompatible with being anti-Catholic), students tell of being told that the Catholic Church was of the devil. "They said the Church had gone over to the world, was decadent and a travesty of Christianity. I was told I had an intellectual belief but I hadn't made it personal, so I would go to hell."[1] The American bishops in their pastoral letter on campus ministry observed that fundamentalist groups employ aggressive proselytizing tactics and promise clear answers and instant security in the midst of a frightening and complex world.

Fears for Catholic Liberals

Reforming fundamentalists fear that contemporary Roman Catholicism will become like the liberal Protestantisms they find empty and unbiblical. This strikes anyone with experience of a Catholic parish or a Vatican congregation as humorous, even fantastic. They fear that Catholicism will cease to have any objective beliefs, any confidence in the history of Jesus, any moral principles. While there are a few American Catholics—theological journalists more than theologians—who live from publicizing daring ideas, Catholic life since Vatican II does not involve reducing the Trinity or the resurrection but focuses rather on church structures (the ordination of women and of married men), liturgical forms, and social and medical ethics. Fundamentalists fear, too, that central authority (which they themselves would not consider obeying at all) is eroding. Catholicism is struggling now with finding a proper balance between papal authority and some participation in church life by bishops, theologians, experts, the baptized. When one ponders the exaggerations of papal authority in Catholic minds, and the role of the pope in determining the agenda and the decisions of all enterprises of bishops, Vatican power is hardly eroding.

The new fundamentalist reformism accuses Catholicism of becoming since Vatican II "liberal" and advocates a return to a "conservative" past. What is not appreciated is that "liberal" and "conservative" mean different things for post-conciliar Catholics in the second half of the twentieth century than they have meant for Protestants. "Liberal" and "conservative" are understood today as describing practical approaches to areas of Christian faith which have concerned Catholics since Vatican II. As we saw, these are themselves largely practical areas like church structure or life (Vatican II was a "pastoral," not a "dogmatic" ecumenical council). Liberal means a willingness to change forms, while conservative is a reluctance to lose a certain ethos or atmosphere connected with forms. Thus, the poles of discussion will concern the limits of legitimate change and the value of certain forms. Precisely history and a sacramental atmosphere engender a church life which is conservative *and* liberal. A respectful questioning of how the Vatican bureaucracy makes decisions in new issues of medical-moral ethics is not the same as challenging the very essence of the power of the bishop of Rome.[2]

This outsider mentoring of Catholicism is conducted under the patronizing guise of concern over the fragility of Catholic life, and is conducted falsely in terms of theological agreement. In fact, it is a campaign to undermine the theological principles of Catholicism (which we will sketch in a later chapter) and to distract the Catholic Church from its identity and mission.

True and False Ecumenisms

True ecumenism is based upon knowledge and love. A Christian tradition should know other traditions, not as they appear in hasty images or tattered prejudices, but as that church has existed in its history, is now, and would like to be. Each Christian church must love the other church; love means permitting something to be what it is, and delighting in discovering that essence and learning from it.

A false ecumenism, on the other hand, is based upon ignorance, fear and aggression. The old fear of Catholicism as a totalitarian superstition has yielded to a new fear of Roman Catholicism as not remaining rigid, authoritarian and monolithic. Ponderous German theologians, conservative American bishops, even the Vatican—all have become "liberals."

As we said, non-Catholic correctors of contemporary Catholicism know relatively little about that which they wish to reform. Not at home in an ecclesiastical world of any complexity, they misjudge appearances and are blind to the underlying reality; they mistake momentary forms for essence. Inexperienced with a church which is old and worldwide, they see diversity as heresy. They cannot locate both authority and freedom in the Roman Catholic Church.

Despite their upward mobility into the better educated, despite the increasing percentage of Catholics at the best schools, their graduate theological educations in Europe and at Harvard, Yale and Chicago, do Catholics still need care, lectures and reform? Does the United States Catholic Church need the reminder that it might be succumbing to the perspectives of German liberal theology from 1870 to 1950? Was what the universal church believed to be the Holy Spirit at Vatican II really Nietzschean chaos?

Sometimes Catholic educators, bishops and other church leaders are blind to the fundamentalism within voices of reform or evangelistic orientation. Phrases of orthodoxy, criticisms of modern excesses, interest in old rubrics and marginal devotions seem good recommendations for those whose enterprises are actually intent upon reforming Catholicism against its own theology of grace, church and society.

Ecumenism means mutual learning. Catholicism was mainly a learner in theology, exegesis and worship during the ecumenical years from 1950 to 1975. Now it seems that Catholicism is also a teacher in the areas of liturgy, American social issues and the role of Christ amid world religions.

European theologians often ask about ecumenism in America. Certainly America made rapid strides ecumenically from 1950 to 1980, with Catholics entering the movement after 1960. Deep-seated anti-Catholic prejudices faded rapidly, while the haughty Catholic institutional rejection of Protestant churches in weddings and joint worship, in civic meetings and Bible study groups, ended. For over a decade ecumenism has faded as a major enterprise, largely because of its successes. Right now the ecumenical scene may not involve so much discussions of doctrinal unity as critiques of fundamentalisms.

Catholics and Protestants should study together Christian fundamentalism. Because of a different and isolated past, Catholics are usually ignorant of the psychology, sociology and theology of fundamentalisms. Perhaps because of their ecumenical good will they are easy victims to the false reformers.

If we look beneath the worries and programs of the new reformers of the Roman Catholic Church, we usually find not only fears of change and new expressions of Christian life, but an anger at being an outsider. For the fundamentalist remains an outsider whenever society changes and the kingdom of God expands through the church—in short, whenever Christianity meets a new historical age. The fundamentalist mind says "no" to incarnating the gospel in new cultures, in new ways. The fundamentalist identifies the permissiveness of modernity with that human freedom, which is for Aquinas the place of grace and the special dignity of being a man or a woman. Sectarians confuse the introverted religious ideas of professors around 1900 with the legitimate diversity of liturgy and church in Africa and Asia for the year 2000. Their search for authority is for an authority which will confirm a private theology. The characteristics of Catholicism (outlined in subsequent chapters) can only annoy the reformers. History discloses diversity, and the interplay of the human and the divine in, for instance, episcopal authority, liturgy and mystical prayer is alien to their faith.

Ultimately the experience of Catholicism is absent. Without experiencing the power and the mysticism of the Catholic ethos, without any obligation to its structures, it is difficult to understand a faith which is more mystical and sacramental than intellectual.

PART TWO

The Catholic Perspective

4

The Psychology of Fundamentalism

*"The major trick or deception of power is to persuade
people they are winning when they are losing."*
                                    MAURICE MERLEAU-PONTY

*"For me to be a saint means to be myself. Therefore the
problem of sanctity and salvation is in fact the problem of
finding out who I am and of discovering my true self."*
                                    THOMAS MERTON

Our second part, "The Catholic Perspective," begins not with
the two chapters on theological motifs but with a brief discussion of
some psychological factors at work. In an incarnational perspective,
the personality is the active recipient of grace and revelation, and so
how we view our life in grace is important. Human psychology is a
facet of the Catholic perspective on life.

Fundamentalism involves not only a theology but also a psychology. Commitment to fundamentalism springs not so much
from prayer and biblical study as from psychological needs. James
Barr writes: "Generally speaking people do not become fundamentalists if they are already well informed about scripture and theology."[1] He suggests that fundamentalism must be met not with
scriptural passages but by showing that psychological and false
theological reasons have led to a systematic misinterpretation of
scripture for the benefit of the sect. What are the signs of fundamentalism's psychological sources? We will look at several—compulsion for certitude, anxiety over diversity—and also at some responses to these. The following pages present a few areas worth
exploring in a psychology of fundamentalism. Psychology is not the
author's field, and the following insights do not claim to be theoreti-
cally or scientifically verified. They come from the author's experience for over two decades teaching in Protestant and Catholic

seminaries and universities. The following ideas come from experiencing forms of fundamentalism in people of all ages, and from pondering the non-fundamentalist theological directions of Catholicism, particularly as radiating from the synthesis of nature and grace in Thomas Aquinas.

The Drive for Certitude

Despite its constant discussion of "what Jesus has accomplished," fundamentalism is very much focused upon what I am doing in order to enter a privileged relationship with God. The issues one sees in fundamentalism are never far from all religion: elitism, the desire for certitude, anxiety before diversity and change, rigidity, compulsive behavior. The perceptive reader of the gospels can note how Jesus observes and preaches against psychological abuses of religion, religion's distortions of God's reign on earth.

Change, uncertainty, levels of truth or goodness in human life bring intense anxiety. As one quickly learns, you can't discuss faith or theology with a fundamentalist. Religion must not be open to different interpretations, to new ideas and practices. This would undermine the search for an inhuman certitude. The compulsion to be, in word and externals, "right" with God is too strong to permit any relaxation. Religious truths and practices are certain—the personality insists that all it touches be certain. A compulsiveness about this phrase or thing, or a fidelity to this church-person beyond his or her public behavior, betrays this drive. Intense, negative emotions and an emphasis upon human guilt and divine anger fuel this compulsion for certitude. The content of Christianity exists to serve the true believer's needs, needs which are often psychological.

The goal of the fundamentalist (we remember fundamentalist missionaries going from door to door) is to convert, not to discuss the interesting differences between Thomas Aquinas and Duns Scotus, or the different eucharistic liturgies of Baghdad or Milan. The right conversions reinforce this evangelist's creed. Before this need for and commitment to certitude in the smallest details, others should just capitulate. Conversion is the total rejection of a past life and the acceptance of a rigid conformity. Compulsion appears as we notice that fundamentalists can't leave people alone, can't stop arranging other lives and worlds according to one pattern. To resist this compulsion for single-minded neatness is to risk condemnation.

Fundamentalists read only their own books, only their own translations of the Bible (which are often inaccurate paraphrases). The chosen text may not be the Bible but the sermons or logical treatises of a medieval scholar or a Protestant reformer. The printed word is so important, and books offer clarity and proof. What is disturbing is not just heresy or immorality; it is uncertainty. Knowledge is dangerous. Why? Because it makes things complicated. Knowledge brings access to life; knowledge is complex because God's and our histories are rich. The fundamentalist scholar is an apologetic researcher, reluctant to study history or theology, except to refute it.

How important it is to recognize the difference between a stance which is conservative and one which is fundamentalist. To be conservative is to wish to retain the best elements of something with a past, to move slowly toward change. All human beings in some way and at some time are conservative. A leftist politician may prefer Bach's counterpoint. Religion tends to be conservative, as would a large and old institution like the Catholic Church. Jesus aimed for a union of tradition and prophecy. When an individual selects not the past but some symbol of the past, when preserving implies the condemnation of everything different, when all other perspectives about life are clearly wrong, the move is being made toward fundamentalism. The inability to accept diversity and history is significant here. While one can prefer a lengthy, solemn eucharist, a Catholic is not free to shun other legitimate forms of mass, e.g. in a hospital room, in a stadium, in a prison. Condemnation and exclusivism mark the fear-filled prison of a fundamentalist stance. Fundamentalism is not a conservative attitude, for it rejects every past but the one it rigidly honors.

In the "Age of Anxiety"

Some decades ago, W.H. Auden, Leonard Bernstein and Edward Hopper wrote a poem, composed a symphony, painted a picture depicting our times as an "age of anxiety." The role of therapists and the sales of Valium indicate that we still live in that age. Anxiety is a deep uncertainty, disturbing but often scarcely felt. This subtle, debilitating fear questions the direction and limits of my individual personality. Our world is anxious. Americans are numb from change and tired of uncertainty about meaning, society and morality.

Fundamentalism is often born of personal anxiety. Anxiety, existentialist psychologies and philosophies tell us, is not fear, not the fear of this or that object, e.g. a rapist with a gun, a letter of dismissal. Anxiety is a gnawing, fearful unpleasantness. Its object —what we vaguely fear—is generally unclear, repressed.

Anxiety fears limits. Since we (and everything in the universe) are limited, therapists cannot deal with anxiety by removing the cause, all our limitations. Anxiety does diminish as we learn to accept limits. Acceptance of limits would seem to be easy. A calm acquiescence to our individuality, to our humanity, even to our sinfulness, however, is not easy. There is some primal movement in us which aims at doing everything, at being like God (the only being capable of entertaining forms of limitlessness). Acceptance of limits is not the acceptance of mediocrity but the acceptance of our own life, of who we really are. To the extent we understand and approve the contours of our personality and the goals of our legitimate desires we are less anxious. At this point the fundamentalist personality becomes uncomfortable. How dare we talk about "our" life (our age, our culture)! Isn't this insulting to the demanding God? Shouldn't we camouflage our lives with religious slogans? The anxious person thinks that limitations will imprison—but in fact they liberate. The German poet Goethe concluded that precisely in limitations the healthy person finds the context for a work or a life to unfold.

Anxiety and compulsion have a horror of history and diversity. The seasons of human life inevitably involve ambiguity, change and imperfection. Anxiety wants to be distinctly right, sublimely certain in morality and religion. The fundamentalist personality fights off anxiety by avoiding diversity or change which it identifies as relativistic, imperfect, and hence dangerous before a divine standard of what is right. Change fans the fires of anxiety, while certitudes calm them. To appease anxiety, special words ("Jesus is Lord") must be venerated; doctrines must not be interpreted (biblical inspiration or millenarianism—a thousand years of rural peace on earth); rituals must be fixed. Finally, anxiety will be present in the religion of an angry God because that religion may claim too much: to be new and yet solely Christian, to offer the miraculous, to be unique and superior.

There can be no diversity, past or present, in Christianity. For variety unleashes the anxiety born of not being absolutely certain. Hence fundamentalists do not like to learn about the past: the past displays diverse and limited ways of understanding Christ, church, justification by faith and grace. Nervous believers are dismayed when they visit the catacombs in Rome to find out that there were people called "popes" in the third century and that Christians were then interested in the eucharist, dismayed not just because these recall Catholicism, but because they indicate that other forms of Christianity have lived in history. Fundamentalists do not want to hear about what is different. They find it particularly painful to learn of the Eastern Orthodox liturgy and understanding of Christianity. This is all too different from a rural American church to be divinely approved. How unsettling to learn that it is so widespread and so old.

Doubtless many Protestant fundamentalists find fulfillment in their Christian faith. We can notice, however, how psychological drives produce some types of unhappy, unfulfilled personalities.

There are (1) the fundamentalists as judges. Preaching on television or engaging in a neighborhood conversation, these persons, simply by their creed or church, embrace being constituted a religious, moral judge of other human beings. There are (2) the fundamentalists as the inmates of a mental monastery. Being uncomfortable with culture and history, they separate themselves from daily life. Ordinary events are reduced to the battlegrounds of angels and demons. Biblical prophecies or Marian visions bring reality. There are (3) the fundamentalists as apocalyptic avengers. These individuals' misfortunes fuel the desire to see humanity worsening. History expects a divine condemnation. If one's own life is sad, should not the world be evil? Fundamentalism can often lead believers to prefer worldwide Armageddon to being wrong in South Dakota. Sadly we see these psychologies at work in the programs of televangelists who delight in musing over a burning, catastrophic end to humanity—a fitting reward for an America of viewers not contributing enough money. Finally there are (4) the purist fundamentalists who shut their ears or rend their garments against the blasphemy of other views. In politics as in religion some people become agitated when faced with several reasonable viewpoints. They cannot bear even to hear ideas questioning their prognoses or statistics which suggest that people are prospering without their message. The agitation that they might be wrong becomes more and more unnerving.

The fundamentalist psyche has various trajectories, contours and goals. Sometimes one hears beneath the impassioned "Christian" slogans and wonders the unspoken ecstasy, "I am a star." But at other times one detects, "I must not rest." The fundamentalist hopes that religious certitudes will bring an end to this rapid oscillation between being everything and being nothing. No matter how much the fundamentalist may talk about Jesus as Lord or God as miracle-worker, it becomes evident that this person is really the center of the religious universe, and that faith is summoned to support a fragile ego in a shifting world.

The Quest of Youth

Young people are in the midst of a life which has begun but whose identity is not yet clear. Faced with choices and demands, their optimism and energy may flag, and they may be drawn to religious remedies—healthy or unhealthy—for their uncertainties and fears.

Recently I was asked advice by a young man about to enter a new, reactionary quasi-religious order. Only a few years in existence, it was adorned with antiquarian customs but with few effective ministries; it was not approved by the Catholic Church. I gained the impression that he, inexperienced in religious life and ignorant of the great religious orders like the Jesuits or Franciscans, saw himself as already superior to most people in the church. Somewhere, someone had imparted to him the conviction that he and the little association founded a few years ago by middle-age Catholics with an elitist agenda were superior to all other religious orders. A young person enters a cult, an unapproved seminary or an unhealthy novitiate for a variety of reasons. This new way (religious clothes of the nineteenth century, automatic rituals, little thinking or ministry) is the only way; there is a gulf between the special route they have chosen and the world. Others have fallen away from perfection. Young fundamentalists in cultic groups rarely stay long and upon departure often embrace eventually the standards of the world they rejected.

Where does this rigidity come from? Fear and compulsion should be foreign to youth. Why are young people today drawn to fundamentalisms of various sorts? Does it come from the parents? There can be influence from fundamentalist parents on their children. But, as novels and movies like to narrate, the opposite effect often happens; youth from a too religious home rebel. More often, however, parents are probably influential in an "indirect" way. How children experience their parents over twenty years may instill primal emotions: fear or love, anxiety or hope. Parental images influence our image of God as do our experiences of teachers, priests, and evangelists. The mother and father touch the child's development. An economically unstable household can bring a longing for security; a violent alcoholic parent can suggest a horrified rejection of any beer or wine.

Unlike the previous generation, young people have been raised in an era of change, in society and in the church. They have seen the phony impotence of some liberalisms and have rejected the comfortable liberal Christianity where nothing ultimately must be held by faith or lived by moral decision. Thus they are looking for a faith which involves reality and commitment. This quest can lead to a mature faith with different levels and to charity, or to the rigidity and elitism of a fundamentalism.

Protestant (and Catholic) fundamentalisms do prey upon young people. They use fear, elitism, false certitudes as instruments of conversion. Many young Christians are drawn to these groups because they are healthily interested in a deeper form of faith and life. They search for Christian community but are offered parishes which are impersonally large, too filled with abstract preaching. An expectation that there are absolutes in ethics and revelation may have been dismissed by ministers and theologians for whom Christianity is little more than a psychology.

Young people fall into fundamentalism sometimes because they are frightened of the future, frightened of the lifelong mission to discover who they are amid the silent inspirations of the Holy Spirit. Fundamentalism responds to their compulsion toward certainty and perfection, or their anger at weakness or arrogance around them. They cannot leave rigidity, although they may leave all religion if ever they abandon fundamentalism.

When one talks to a young person involved in fundamentalism, one senses that their own (meager) experience of life is very active. The young personality, however, seems to be both too strong and too weak: too strong in relentlessly cultivating and defending an unchallenged, immature image of a demanding God; too weak to overcome the rigidity of a personality insecure with its capabilities and life's demands. Thus it seeks absolutes in religious things and words.

Like young people, athletes are drawn to fundamentalism.

Sports put them under pressure to win, to succeed in this shot or play. They need power and success in an instant. So much—winning, fame, self-worth, money—is riding upon a single physical action that it is understandable that the supranatural would be invoked to direct miraculously the pass or the kick to its desired goal. Young athletes, for whom the game is the world, are drawn to an enthusiastic circle who advocate dedication and self-confidence.

Fundamentalist groups are cheerleaders for the miraculous intervention of God. In fact, the miraculous is rare. God's kingdom is concerned with deeper human issues, all human issues. Silent grace touches the contours of life all the time. Sports are a game depending upon human abilities and contingent factors and not a showplace for supernatural powers. Thomas Aquinas observed that God's glory comes from making us true causes of what we do. Prayer can request God's invisible and unmiraculous power to be present in the depths of our life, but it would go against the very nature of a game to expect miraculous intervention. A place-kicker, who had won an important game in the last seconds, expressed a mature theology: "I pray that the best thing be done—and kick the ball like hell!" Prayer in sports, as in every facet of our life, asks for God's hidden and unperceived inspiration and help, but the sign of the cross does not arouse a sleeping saint or angel to accomplish wonders.

Images of Welcome; Masks of Anger

Every faith faces the question of who is God. Every person faces the issue of who is God for me. Religion sometimes makes us afraid of God and angry at ourselves.

Fearful Before an Angry God. Our deepest attitudes toward God are fashioned from our imagination of God. Images and emotions join together. We can hear a dozen sermons, pray hourly, study theology, but it will all have little effect if our image of God holds the opposite theological psychology. If you imagine God to be strict and angry, or if you have concluded that God is hostile to a large part of the human race, you will remain afraid of God. This God who is a strict judge must be appeased, made to smile briefly by accepting narrow religious ideas. Outside this God and this religion lies their wrath, hell.

There is some sickness deep inside of us which distorts our image of God and of self. This illness is a sign of original sin, of the "fallen condition" of the human race. We readily fashion ugly, fearful masks for God. But the masks are not God's face or personality but projections of evil, injury, despair upon the true God who opposes them. False images of God making us afraid are prominent in our psychological life.

Images of God influence our social and familial life. We may learn to behave as if we must trick God who will then reward us, children, in a condescending way. Business, politics, the military, schools, even the churches are conducted as if some despot rules an empire of slaves. This distant being demands appeasement, adulation, achievement. Moreover, the leaders of government, university, business and church sometimes appear to be men and women haunted by some higher power making impossible and tiring demands of them. Thus human beings meet and invite false images of God into their personality and give them control of their lives.

Figures like Marx or Freud in our century have claimed that Christianity nourishes and furthers unhealthy images of God. Have we made God into a merciless banker always examining the balance of our life or into an envious partner who begrudges us our own talents? The image we have of God corresponds to the image we have of our own self. It is difficult to free ourselves from false images of God! That is why people—even religious people—fear death and what lies beyond death so much.

A hostile god implies bad people. But we are not evil people. The New Testament argues that God is a God of love and mercy, not of judgment and punishment. Paul and Thomas Aquinas presume that into the believer's life the Spirit of Jesus enters. The Christian is not a bomb waiting to explode or a bundle of selfishness but a living person whom the Spirit loves so much that God's love works out our love. Of course, I remain a sinner, too open to selfishness and self-delusion, but love and life, not fear and suspicion, are the faces of God, of Jesus the Christ and of our own graced self.

A Catholic critique of fundamentalism's psychological dimension includes a critique of how we experience and imagine God. Hans Küng observes that the God Jesus preached is not a God of the hereafter at the expense of the here and now, at the expense of human creativity and achievement, not a God of the ruling classes or of unjust social conditions, not a God which encourages childish religion, magical superstition, the appeasement of fears. Jesus' image of God is revolutionary: his Father proclaims a higher law which is love, a sacred righteousness which evaluates even organized religion in terms of its service to people.[2] This God makes his kingdom but also men and women to be the standard of his commandments. Religion exists to serve people; people do not exist to run the sweatshops and museums of religion.

Anger Calls to Anger. The perceptive television viewer may note that the evangelists on TV often project anger. Anger rises up because the evangelist's personality is becoming tired of performance, tired of achieving. If my gospel alone claims to have the truth in an evil world, if my church—no matter how small or new it may be—is the only "ministry" of the Holy Spirit, I have an impossible responsibility. At first I am a star, but eventually I become a casualty.

If your salvation now and in the future depends on a small group being right, you too would be angry at any challenge to that message and that group. Since I have access to God, lack of respect for my church is an insult to God.

Compulsions bring fatigue and eventually anger at this burden; the same is true with constant anxiety. Eventually the strong personality reaches limits and impossible demands. William Packard sees "frenzy" as a component of fundamentalist preaching.[3] Evangelism from tent shows to television surrounds the gospel with exciting forms: miracles, prophecies of doom, observations of evil everywhere in society. This builds to a frenzy and makes it good theater as excitement moves toward the miraculous, the awaited and supernatural coming of the Spirit now and Jesus soon. But frenzy and the miraculous exhaust; they do not resolve anxiety and uncertainty but only numb them and call for more excitement.

Intensity and zeal, obedience and commitment do not necessarily bring anger. Pressure brings anger. The preacher is under tremendous pressure to prove that he or she is God's prophet. To be successful, to attract attention, the preacher must confirm God's approval through miracles and money. The evangelist must vindicate that his or her theology is God's revelation and that miracles are being worked, both physical and economic. Anyone who lives each day under such pressures as these—to be better than others, to know the mind of God, to be God's agent of miracles—would become angry and afraid. Daily life is hard enough, but imagine if the day demanded cures of cancer or raising from the anonymous electronic church beyond your cameras a million dollars in a week. Who would not be angry at and afraid of the demanding God? These emotions explain partly the temptations to drugs, possessions and sex; they dampen the impossible demands.

Catholic theologian Richard McBrien agrees that psychological orientations and problems lie at the source of fundamentalisms. He develops this theme succinctly by asking a number of questions:

> Why is certitude so important to some religious people, and why do they expect it, even demand it in religion? What accounts for their own sense of moral and intellectual certitude? Are they really as certain inside as they seem to be on the outside? Do they ever have serious doubts about their faith? How do they handle those doubts? At what psychological cost?
>
> Why are they not satisfied simply to rebut their foes

and to show the weakness of error of their views? Why do they seem so eager to punish as well, e.g. by getting a person fired from a job or trying to besmirch the person's reputation? Most people don't enjoy kicking another human being in the teeth. Do aggressive religious people get pleasure out of it? Do they ever feel guilty about it later? Does their behavior toward other people reflect in any way upon their own self-esteem?[4]

Considerable anger and resentment lie in people caught in fundamentalist certitude and intolerance. Why do they feel left out? Left out of what? Is the root of their anxiety really a lack of faith, or guilt over a period in which they abandoned religious faith? And, finally, there is another question where theology and psychology meet: why the preoccupation with sex and the lack of concern for poverty, racism and injustice?

The Pain and Health of the Middle

Both psychology and Christianity advocate living in the "middle." For Christianity this is not the middle of relativism or mediocrity, but the middle of faith and incarnation. We are not God, and what we know of God comes through faith. Our world is not filled with miracles although Jesus asked us to fill it with ordinary charity.

Fundamentalists seek a divine world. Their ideas about God and religion never change; divinely approved, they are superior to those of all others. The healthy world of the middle, however, accepts limitations. It knows it can control neither one individual life nor the entire universe. It seeks a remedy for its anxieties not in power but in faith, hope and the welcome love of others. In the world of the kingdom of God judgment is not prominent. Since the incarnation is an affirmation of our race on earth there is no mandate to condemn people. Christianity does not command severity and damnation toward billions. God's grace is capable of reaching those who have never heard of Jesus or who cannot comprehend that he is the light of the world.

The middle is where the divine and the human, grace and

personality, Christ and myself meet. There each has its legitimate expectations; each spotlights the "new law" of love. The bond between the divine and the human is not justice or achievement but mercy. We will ponder in the next chapters how the interplay of the human and the divine exists in Catholicism. The incarnation reaches beyond the sacraments to encompass human life, art, nature and society. Like the incarnation, the redemptive death and resurrection of Christ exists in the middle where the human can meet in faith the reality of God's love in history.

The Quiet Response

Often any response we bring to a fundamentalist meets rejection; even agreeing with basic premises that secular theology is self-contradictory and that liberal relativism is injurious meets rejection. Only the response of complete conversion and submission is enough. A fundamentalism—in politics as well as in religion—is a strict club with a correct jargon and elite overseers.

A quiet response to the fears and drives of the fundamentalist psyche involves three "theological therapies": dissolving false images of God through the teaching of Jesus, letting be, and hope.

We must not nourish the false image of God we have consciously or unconsciously absorbed from life. One of Jesus' great lessons in his parables is that God is different from the pictures sketched by organized religion: different in the sense that God is more generous, more loving. Christianity preaches not a severe divine mind but an outreach of God called "the kingdom of God" or "love" or "grace." This incarnation says "yes" to the human, and so says "yes" to life, to culture, to history. Sometimes Christianity can give the impression that faith simply means watching a biblical pageant where semitic figures in the first century act out a play unrelated to our own times. But from the New Testament we learn that the Spirit of Jesus is not a magician at the beck and call of a few charismatics. The Spirit has larger plans, greater tasks, millions of recipients to contact. The Spirit in individuals and social movements continues the work of Jesus' preaching and resurrection.

A second, psychological response to fundamentalism is found in the phrase "letting be." This is not a line from people who have no commitment but a psychological theology from great Christian mystics. We must let be, not in the sense of having no commitment but by letting God and ourselves be what each is destined to be. To let God be God is to give God the permission to love even those who do not know him; to let God be God is not to imprison this deity in some thing or place.

Dare I let myself be? Fundamentalism is frequently the repression of individual life; everything is believed and done because of threats and rewards, commands and voices. But the individual is drowning. For many people it is difficult to be a major actor in their own life. The demands made by parents and authorities, by the false spectres of God, the attraction of endless activity, or the thrill of running organizations of people are so strong that they stifle the self. William Lynch wrote:

> Thus it is necessary for the human being to move progressively from a solipsistic world, where he uses only his own mind, to a world where he puts on the minds of others in an increasingly public act of thinking and imagining. . . . This involves many acts of trust and faith . . . (and) explains the process of religious faith itself because whether or not we accept the process in the concrete, it is nothing more than putting on still another mind, this time the mind of God, with which to see reality.[5]

Thomas Merton observes the link between creation and redemption and does not hesitate to state that "for me to be a saint means to be myself. Therefore the problem of sanctity and salvation is in fact the problem of finding out who I am and of discovering my true self."[6] Endowed with activity and freedom we can choose a variety of selves, some of them false selves embedded within us by original sin. "The problem is this: since God alone possesses the secret of my identity, he alone can make me who I am or rather, he alone can make me who I will be when I at last fully begin to be. *The seeds that are planted in my liberty at every moment, by God's will, are the seeds of my own identity, my own reality, my own happiness, my own sanctity.*"[7] We may be shocked by the four words—"identity," "reality," "happiness," "sanctity"—being equated. Religion has often separated them, pitted them against each other. But, Merton is noting, if there is one God, then the healthy side of my personality will not be at war with the sanctity to which God's grace is inviting me. Moreover, even if I become a "star," or a "genius," or a "millionaire," or a "church leader," and that is not my identity and reality and sanctity, I have become something which God never intended me to be, and someone who I do not want to be.

Third, we ask: Is every fundamentalism born of an absence of hope? Is it born of a secret fear that God is not there? The demands upon others and upon self, the elaborate rituals and self-congratulatory ministries, the denunciations of others, betray an absence of hope. And as time passes, the absence of hope fuels anger. The devotee comes to realize that the world will not submit to his or her will as an orchestra follows its conductor. Hope includes more than optimism and activity. There must be hope not only in our belief and energy, but hope in others. Sometimes we will hope in change, even hope in institutions (for most people live in institutions). Above all, we hope in God; the Christian virtue of hope, reaching from this moment into the next life, is a hope in the silent power of God.

So fundamentalism is, in its own way, a search for God, and a search for self-identity. Fundamentalisms and the Catholic understanding of Christianity differ over the extent to which we take our personalities seriously, the degree in which we criticize poor images of self and of God. Everyone fears being alone. If God is strict and if people are evil, one is indeed alone! Christmas, Good Friday, Easter—their message is not that we must appease an angry God but that a God of love has found us, has embraced our humanity with its diversity and its dirt, with its achievements and its wanderings. When the incarnation of the word of God in Jesus is understood in the traditional and orthodox way, it advocates the affirmation of self and the pursuit of a healthy psychology, for the grace of God has decided to work through people.

What must interest us in biblical revelation is not an end of the world drawn in the colors of science fiction but the hope and suffer- ing of the real world, now and in the future. Our faith in God must reach the level of intensity where it banishes all that is debilitating in religion, and where it encourages the slow emergence of my own identity. For that identity fashions and narrates my own self, a unique person whom God—out of an eternal plan which is wis- dom and generosity—has loved into human existence and divine friendship.

5

Catholic Critics

"The clouds of heaven thunder forth throughout the world that God's house is being built. But these frogs sit in their pond and croak: 'We're the only Christians.'"

ST. AUGUSTINE

"Nobody with a good car needs to be justified."

HAZEL MOTES
IN FLANNERY O'CONNOR'S "WISE BLOOD"

God's presence of grace enters into a human life; this presence draws a personality to its deepest life and its special destiny. So, in the spirit of this perspective of Thomas Aquinas and western Catholicism we have begun with psychology. Now two chapters present the Catholic understanding of Christianity with its various contrasts to the fundamentalist mind.

This chapter gathers ideas and viewpoints from Roman Catholics with different fields of expertise. Then Chapter 6 highlights characteristics of the Catholic mind and community.

Four sources begin this Catholic critique and perspective. Richard McBrien is a university theologian but also the writer of a weekly column and a television commentator on religion and American politics. To introduce ideas touching the New Testament we have Raymond Brown, a well-known exegete who teaches at a Protestant seminary, Union Theological Seminary in Manhattan. The American Catholic bishops, startled by the prominence of Protestant fundamentalism, wrote a pastoral letter on the topic. Finally, we conclude not with theology but with literature. For a vivid, sometimes paradoxical and shocking Catholic understanding of American religion, including its fundamentalist forms, one cannot find anyone more insightful than the novelist and short-story writer, Flannery O'Connor.

Cultural Theologian: Richard McBrien

We will look at Richard McBrien's evaluation of fundamentalism through ideas drawn from his popular weekly columns, and then turn to his theology of how Catholicism differs essentially from fundamentalism. In a number of columns after 1985 he has examined aggressive fundamentalism.

> Fundamentalism may be the most immediate threat to Catholic faith in the United States today. Some of the television evangelists—all Protestant fundamentalists—boast that as much as 30 percent of their financial support comes from Catholic viewers. In fact, when Jimmy Swaggart recently criticized certain points of Catholic doctrine, including the papacy, his fellow preachers urged him to back off for fear of alienating their Catholic supporters. He did not, by the way. Thousands of Catholics belong to fundamentalist Bible study groups and flock to preaching-and-pray services in convention centers and outdoor stadiums all across the United States.[1]

Catholics who are involved in Protestant fundamentalism often do not see the contradictions in their stance. Not only does fundamentalism by its very nature exclude church authority and much of liturgy, but many fundamentalist leaders and groups are implicitly or explicitly anti-Catholic. "Catholics who are fundamentalists cannot have it both ways: bemoaning the erosion of traditional, orthodox Catholicism, while throwing in their own spiritual lot with those who reject basic Catholic dogmas as unbiblical and, therefore, false."[2]

The Notre Dame theologian distinguishes between "biblical" and "doctrinal" fundamentalisms. While both are found in fundamentalist groups outside the Roman Catholic Church, "doctrinal fundamentalism" can exist inside the Catholic Church when a member insists that a church stance be interpreted only in one way, or when a Catholic prefers a view of society or grace which is hostile to Catholic theological tradition.

Texts from scripture (or from the church) are the battleground of fundamentalist interpretation. Every fundamentalism is an assertion of private interpretation and a denial of continuing, church interpretation. But the church, as Vatican documents argue, finds the meaning of the pronouncements of faith partly in the expressive power of the language used at a certain point in history and in particular circumstances. For the fundamentalist, however, "interpretation is unnecessary because the meaning of the text is self-evident."[3] The contribution of experts in science or history, of theologians, even of the teaching church, is irrelevant.

Fr. McBrien has achieved considerable success by describing the deeper nature of Catholicism for a church living amid renewal, change and ecumenism. Western Catholicism is a form of the Christian faith and also a way of being human. "The Catholic Church is a community of persons (the fundamentally *human* foundation of Catholic identity) that believes in, and is committed to, the reality of God, and shapes its life according to that belief and in fidelity to that commitment (the *religious* component of Catholicism). The Church's belief in, and commitment to, the reality of God is focused in its fundamental attitude towards Jesus Christ (the *Christian* core)."[4]

To be a Catholic, McBrien notes, is a way of being human even as it is a way of understanding God active in religion, in all of human life. "Catholicism is an understanding and affirmation of human existence before it is a corporate conviction about the pope, or the seven sacraments, or even about Jesus Christ." McBrien singles out three characteristics of Catholicism; they are influential aspects of faith in Jesus as the incarnate word of God which influence the way Catholics see their religious world and their life.

> There is a configuration of characteristics within Catholicism that is not duplicated anywhere else in the community of Christian churches. This configuration of characteristics is expressed in Catholicism's theology; its body of doctrines, its liturgical life, especially the Eucharist; its variety of spiritualities, its religious congregations and lay apostolates; its official teachings on justice, peace and human rights; its exercise of collegiality; and, to be sure, its Petrine ministry. Catholicism is distinguished from the

Christian traditions and churches in its understanding of,
commitment to, and exercise of, the principles of sacramentality, mediation and communion.

The *sacramental* view "sees" or "feels" God in and through
things. "The visible, the tangible, the finite, the historical—all these
are actual or potential carriers of the divine presence. Indeed, for
the Catholic it is only in and through these material realities that we
can even encounter the invisible God." If matter and cosmos can be
bearers of grace, as can the spiritual schools and liturgical rites of
different cultures, the world, though fallen, is essentially good. Like
the plan of salvation in Christ, the universe comes from a wise and
good plan of God.

There are concentric circles of sacramentality: at the center is
Jesus of Nazareth where the divine being is a Jewish man; then
there are eucharist, baptism and the other sacraments; the liturgy or
decoration of the church and creation itself are places where "grace
(the divine presence) actually enters into and transforms nature
(human life in its fullness)." Human nature is not always ugly or
decrepit, at war with God's grace, but rather human existence re-
ceives and lives from God's special presence we call "grace." The
history of the world is, at the same time, the history of salvation.

Mediation extends sacramentality. "A sacrament not only signifies; it also causes what it signifies . . . sacraments cause grace
precisely insofar as they signify it." So created things, sacraments
and church, not only reflect and recall the activity of a saving
Father, Lord and Spirit, they make it present, accessible, even effective.

Communion explains the prominence of the church, not just of
the pope but of local churches, different ministries, liturgies in a
hospital room or cathedral, in architecture and social action. "For
Catholicism the mystery of the Church has always had a significant
place in its theology, doctrine, pastoral practice, moral vision and
devotion. Catholics have always emphasized the place of the
Church as the sacrament of Christ which mediates salvation
through sacraments and ministries and other institutional elements
and forms." This characteristic explains the perduring ethnic char-
acter of Catholicism, the extended family of the communion of

saints, the ability to adjust to new cultures. Far from being mono-form and rigid, Catholic parishes and dioceses are quite diverse.

These three facets—sacramentality, mediation and church communion—are at the root of why Catholicism interprets Christianity differently from fundamentalism. They are more important than a biblical text or a medal's blessing.

Biblical Expert: Raymond Brown

Raymond Brown has been a particular target of fundamentalists perhaps because of his union of creativity and balance. He sees fundamentalism as an attempt to bend the person and teaching of Jesus to serve one thing: religious security. "Fundamentalism is saying, 'You really don't have to think—this ancient document or statement is your answer, all set for you.' One forgets that human beings wrote the Bible and that human beings received it. The biblical message was closely related to the human situation of thousands of years ago. It will be comprehended in another situation, which is ours, only if we see what it meant to the situation in which it was first written."[5]

The response to fundamentalism is not to summon forth new theories to which scholars may have given their own infallibility, although the historical-critical method tells us when and under what circumstances a book was written, and what the author meant. Nor is the response to fundamentalism a skepticism about every faith and a suspicion that religion is delusion. Biblical pages should help us appreciate the human and the divine in revelation's record, scripture.

Television and radio transmit dozens of figures shrilly announcing the details of the end of the world. Fr. Brown observes:

I think that most of the people explaining *Revelation* (or *Apocalypse*) haven't the slightest idea that the book is not dealing with the distant future. Often the media preachers completely misunderstand the genre or type of literature written in the first century. The biblical writer did not have any clear idea about when the world was going to end . . . rather, he was using figurative language. Thus, such media preaching is a misunderstanding of apocalyptic literature ... and this interpretation produces a distorted religion because people spend their time figuring out signs and numbers. The chief message of Christianity does not consist in knowing the exact details of the end of the world. That's not what Jesus came to proclaim. As a matter of fact, there are very few specifics about the future in Jesus' preaching other than that God is going to accomplish his purpose and he's going to accomplish it through Jesus.

Some fundamentalist media stars, however, are engaged not in prophesying immediate doom but in selling a pop psychology aimed at producing in their audience the feeling of being "OK," of having a chance at health and wealth in every circumstance. But, Brown responds, Jesus did not make people more secure. He certainly was not a marketer of ideas for becoming wealthy, or a miraculous purveyor of immortality in *this* life. "Jesus challenged people, and, indeed, shook some of their securities. His greatest opposition in fact came from religious people."

A Pastoral Letter from the American Catholic Bishops

In 1987 the American bishops composed a pastoral letter on the topic of this book, addressing it to "our Catholic brothers and sisters who may be attracted to biblical fundamentalism without realizing its serious weaknesses."[6]

The bishops too begin with a psychological profile. "Fundamentalism indicates a person's general approach to life which is typified by unyielding adherence to rigid doctrinal and ideological positions." The bishops note the attraction, particularly with young people, of zealous Christians concerned with religion influencing family life and politics and promising certitude and personal conviction. The attempt to find in the Bible all the answers for life today (the Bible nowhere claims such authority) is understandable. "Our world is one of war, violence, dishonesty, personal and sexual irresponsibility. . . . People of all ages yearn for answers. They look for sure, definite rules for living. And they are given answers—simplistic answers to complex issues—in a confident and enthusiastic way in fundamentalist Bible groups."

The bishops' letter, while noting a doctrinal fundamentalism (our approach), addresses only biblical fundamentalism. There the Bible is presented as a sufficient "single rule" to the exclusion of the teaching church with "its creeds and other doctrinal formulations, its liturgical and devotional traditions." Despite the centrality of the Bible (the bishops wish to increase the prominence of the scriptures in liturgy, preaching and religious education), from the Catholic perspective, the church offers the context and the living interpretation of the pages of the Bible. "The church produced the New Testament. . . . The New Testament did not come before the church but from the church. The first generation of Christians had no New Testament at all—but they were the church then, just as we are the church today." While the focus of this brief letter is fundamentalism in its biblical form, the bishops stress that most fundamentalist groups do not accept or encourage central aspects of Catholic faith and life—the eucharist and other sacraments, the liturgy of the Christian year, the authority of the church, the social teachings of present-day Catholicism.

The bishops' letter is brief and leaves for further consideration theological issues which speak to "doctrinal fundamentalism," distinctly Catholic areas of faith which fundamentalists reject.

Writer: Flannery O'Connor

Flannery O'Connor's world was paradoxical. She was a masterful writer and well-read in theology. She was a Catholic living in the rural Protestant south. Her observations of the exuberant faith and religion of the southern social levels were perceptive but sympathetic, kind even when she permitted the characters of her short stories to walk into religion's foibles and danger.

There is no lack of observers who have pointed out the "sacramental" nature of O'Connor's fiction where tattooed backs and violent deaths may be revealing the gospel. Life is definitely not lived away from a distant God in a neutral state where sin has been scrubbed clean. "From my own experience in trying to make stories 'work', I have discovered that what is needed is an action that is totally unexpected, yet totally believable, and I have found that for me, this is always an action which indicates that grace has been offered. And frequently it is an action in which the devil has been the unwilling instrument of grace. . . . My subject in fiction is the action of grace in territory held largely by the devil."[7]

What shocks many is how religion is portrayed. There are dangerous pictures. In *The River* a child is so entranced with the ritual of baptism by immersion that it returns to the river to drown. Religion can be maddening. Hazel Motes in *Wise Blood* is scarred by the hounding, ever watchful Jesus his grandfather's preaching evoked. For his own "Holy Church of Christ without Christ" he preaches an anti-gospel where "the blind don't see and the lame don't walk and what's dead stays that way," and where "justification" is less interesting than a running Chevrolet.[8] Then, too, religion can be phony as when the Bible salesman in *Good Country People* first seduces a university student, and then, to provide ready cash, steals her artificial leg.

Religion mediates a dimension of reality which is as real as the evils of this world, not just a revealed message but a kind of orientation or force. "The mystery of existence is always showing through the texture of ordinary lives."[9] We meet messengers in people and nature. In *A Circle in the Fire* voices of modern-day angels sing in sacral tones as the woods they have set afire threaten the self-justified, while an interplay of darkness and light begins and ends the descent into the hell of Atlanta redeemed by the grace of forgiveness in *The Artificial Nigger.* In *Revelation* a college student in the waiting room, irritated by Mrs. Turpin's self-righteousness, throws a book at her and calls her "a warthog from hell." This lack of respect leads the stout heroine to demand angrily of God concerning the social diversity of the humans he has made: "Who do you think you are?"[10]

Someone reading Flannery O'Connor for the first time might conclude that she is only a critic of a hypocritical and perverse rural religiosity. Certainly she points out its exaggerations and conflicts. What we call "religion" is simply myriads of ways in which her characters deal with and encounter self, grace and sin. The bizarre struggles of her characters are engaged in the real fabric of human life. At one level the author is concluding that a theology too self-enclosed is dangerous, that some faiths which claim a peaceful Bible or Jesus as their immediate source are as dangerous as a runaway truck loaded with dynamite. But at a deeper level, she seems to be saying that even exaggerated and deformed religion is more in touch with reality than is no religion. Or, in Catholic terms, the ultimate fabric of human life is not the laws of gravity or the curve of interest rates but the inescapable (if unseen) series of meetings and conversations between sin and grace.

John Garvey has observed the "fundamentalist" side of O'Connor's world-view:

> I have always found it interesting that Flannery O'Connor, without moving an inch from her profound Catholic belief, usually chose evangelical, biblically fundamentalist Protestants as her archetypical Christians. This could be because at certain levels—the ones which interested O'Connor, as an artist and as a Christian—the choices we find presented by Christianity really do involve the dramatic either/or decisions, the radical choices emphasized in Swaggart's kind of preaching.[11]

For the southern Catholic writer, the ultimate structure of reality lies amid sin and grace. Evil and sin do exist and choices are painfully necessary and can have serious consequences. "There are times when the choices are between good and evil, God and Satan, life and death, and we would rather avoid this. It makes us embarrassed in a pluralistic culture to say that the culture itself, good as it has been to us, good as it has been for religion, is limited, and our lives finally are not. Flannery O'Connor knew this. Jesus really does present us with hard choices, and they may make us look funny."[12]

Those who in today's mood of liberalism deny the existence of sin and grace, who have used agnosticism as an excuse from seeing the effects of addiction and amorality in people's lives, end up in O'Connor's stories shipwrecked. By not perceiving how sensuality differs from charity, the individual enters a foggy ocean where dangers, like reefs, are not recognized in time. In *The Lame Shall Enter First,* a liberal social worker tries to disabuse a crippled boy, chronically and exuberantly involved in stealing, of his tough Christian convictions, e.g. sin and hell. The boy views his thefts and the social worker's atheism as both sins; the important difference is that the boy knows sin from grace. "I lie and steal because I'm good at it. My foot don't have a thing to do with it! The lame shall enter first! The halt'll be gathered together. When I get ready to be saved, Jesus'll save me, not that lying, stinking atheist."[13]

The following conclusion to the short story *Revelation* illustrates a Catholic theological perspective. After having a book thrown at her, Mrs. Turpin has been spending a day learning that middle-class self-righteousness is not the goal of God's word to us, and that a world divided into social and racial classes is not God's will. Finally the revelation breaks through—a revelation of the ordinariness of grace, of a universal love of God to all kinds of people, of the absence of earning God's pleasure, sinks in.

> Until the sun slipped finally behind the tree lines, Mrs. Turpin remained there with her gaze bent to as if she were absorbing some abysmal life-giving knowledge. At last she lifted her head. There was only a purple streak in the sky, cutting through a field of crimson and leading, like an extension of the highway, into the descending dusk. She raised her hands from the side of the pen in a gesture hieratic and profound. A visionary light settled in her eyes. She saw the streak as a vast swinging bridge, extending upward from the earth through a field of living fire. Upon it a vast horde of souls were rumbling toward heaven. There were whole companies of white-trash, clean for the first time in their lives, and bands of black niggers in white robes, and battalions of freaks and lunatics shouting and clapping and leaping like frogs. And bringing up the end of the procession was a tribe of people whom she recognized at once as those who, like herself and Claud, had always had a little of everything and the God-given wit to

use it right. She leaned forward to observe closer. They were marching behind the others with great dignity, accountable as they had always been for good order and common sense and respectable behavior. They alone were on key. Yet she could see by their shocked and altered faces that even their virtues were being burned away.[14]

Here there is revelation but also human insight, a divine power but also human virtue, salvation in diversity.

Flannery O'Connor found modern secular life more shocking than southern religion. The sharpness of her fiction sets off hidden realities and hidden dangers in the real world. "The novelist with Christian concerns will find in modern life distortions which are repugnant to him, and his problem will be to make these appear as distortions to an audience which is used to seeing them as natural. . . . To the hard of hearing you shout, and for the almost blind you draw large and startling figures."[15]

In her Catholic sacramental orthodoxy and her love of the reality and pain of southern religion, she is a critic of fundamentalism. "The religion of the South is a do-it-yourself religion, something which I as a Catholic find painful and touching and grimly comic. . . . They have nothing to correct their practical heresies and so they work them out dramatically. If this were merely comic to me, it would be no good, but I accept the same fundamental doctrines of sin and redemption and judgment that they do."[16] Her south, populated with comic extremists in the arena of religion, is a place where men and women in their freedom live out their dramas of evil and liberation.

Our four sources have a similar vision, a vision which challenges because it will relinquish neither the human nor the divine. It is neither a secularism from which the mystery of grace has been politely banished, nor a fundamentalist fireworks of miracles. The stance of the middle is healthy both theologically and psychologically—but this perspective makes Catholicism puzzling and difficult. One must be able to hold together emotionally the truths of the gospel in their Jewish context with their new expression in Zaire or Chile, to see in the sacraments both the material and the spiritual, to grasp how church unity can exist within the diversity of hundreds of Roman Catholic religious orders and other institutions.

Following upon these sketches of the Catholic vision, the next chapter, the central one of the book, looks at the basic characteristics of the Catholic interpretation of Christianity, a theology different from that of fundamentalism.

6

The Catholic Perspective

"Christians have much to receive in this dynamic relationship between the church and the contemporary world. The church has been greatly enriched by acquisitions from many civilizations. The secular experience of so many nationalities, the progress of science, the hidden treasures of diverse cultures through which human nature becomes more fully visible, and through which new paths towards the truth open up—all of this is an indisputable advantage for the church."

POPE JOHN PAUL II

Catholicism is the opposite of fundamentalism. In its approach to Christian faith and human life, the Catholic interpretation of Christianity offers a different gospel, an alternative to fundamentalism. Perhaps that explains why Jimmy Swaggart calls it "a false cult." But before we look at the characteristics of Catholic Christianity, we should note why this ongoing incarnational interpretation of Christianity is suited to offer a different perspective.

Problematic Liberalisms

Why are men and women drawn to fundamentalism? One important theological reason is the specter of an exaggerated liberalism. "Liberal" is related to the word "liberty," freedom. To be liberal is to be free: with money, with ideas, with plans for changing things. Every political party, every philosophy or theory of art, every theology has a liberal side attracting men and women who are more open to change than to remaining in a stable, conserving stance.

There must be, however, something to change. Some liberalisms are so free that they no longer have any political platform, any artistic canon of beauty, any content of faith. Total liberalism has as its standard change itself or personal preference.

Fundamentalism is usually occasioned by believers judging religious liberalism to be too fluid, extreme or secular. Has not liberal Christianity wanted to be free not just from slavery to past church forms or injurious theologies but from every dogma or ethic? In its extreme form liberalism ends outside of recognizable religion; it becomes free even of faith and worship.

Without some liberalism a church dies of entropy. Modern Protestant liberalism became dominant in the enlightenment of the eighteenth century, in the new sciences at the end of the nineteenth century, in the existentialism and radical exegesis after two world wars. In each period new fundamentalisms arose. Religion and church are essentially conservative. People draw close to religion and its forms because they need a power and truth beyond them. To abolish the concrete presence of the transcendent and human hope in the divine is to abolish religion. Liberal theology in its unbridled form ends up as psychology. Strangely some liberals who in theory have rejected all of revelation or religion remain in ministry or teaching, spending a lifetime arguing that the history and texts they teach do not mean what they say. So liberal theologies can become fundamentalist when they deny that any interpretation, any set of phrases other than their own, are good or realistic.

Fundamentalism is a shocked revolt at a liberal takeover of faith in the supernatural activity of God. James Barr notes:

> The map of the theological world which fundamentalism disseminates has two major characteristics. First, it is polemical. Other currents in Christianity are seen as an enemy which is seeking to obscure or to destroy the truth; every effort must be made to discredit this enemy and prevent him from receiving any sort of open or sympathetic hearing among the faithful. Secondly, it is extremely simple. . . . Generally speaking most fundamentalist argument is directed against liberals and is therefore valid and effective only if it is true that the non-fundamentalist is really a liberal.[1]

A reaction against an ultimately anti-religious liberalism is un-derstandable. Fundamentalism wants to reassert the legitimacy of faith, the central beliefs of Christianity in the incarnation of God in people's lives. So—and this is important—this book cannot attack fundamentalism from an ultra-liberal position. The answer to fun-damentalism's strong faith cannot be no faith; the response to the advocacy of a transformed life cannot be a secular dismissal of the supernatural's possibility of existing at all. The critique of funda-mentalism's easy identification of the gospel with a rightist political program cannot continue the illusions of academics on both coasts that religion faded away long ago and plays no role in politics (ignoring Chicago, Tulsa, Belfast, Cairo, Lagos, Gdansk).

Fundamentalism's sibling rivalry with extreme liberalism ex-plains why Catholicism is suited to compose this critique of funda-mentalism. Catholicism's theological history in the centuries of modernity, 1750 to 1950, is different from that of liberal Protestant-ism. Affirming a supernatural revelation and faith is strong in Catholicism, a church committed to the traditional dogmas of Christianity.

Catholicism too must have liberal theologians, bishops, charis-matic leaders in Catholicism's understanding of these terms. There are always in the history of Christianity charismatics, visionaries, prophets, activists and thinkers necessarily pushing against the constraints of a church in danger of becoming a museum. Catholi-cism is simultaneously liberal and conservative; its many institu-tions, theologies, traditions and religious orders insure this. Its posi-tive attitude toward culture and psyche permits both newness and history.

"Liberal" and "conservative" have a different meaning in Catholicism since Vatican II. Pierre Teilhard de Chardin and Dan-iel Berrigan would certainly qualify as liberals. Teilhard could ar-guably claim the prize for being the most imaginative theologian of our century with his attempt to show how evolution not only on earth but in the entire universe can be a form extending the histori-cal life of Christ through time and universe. Berrigan, empowered by an early reading in the 1950s of the liberal French Catholic theologians who would contribute so much to Vatican II, has for over a quarter of a century, in prison and out, argued for defense and foreign policies which would take seriously the horror, the avoidance of war. Both Jesuits were silenced by the hierarchy of the church. Neither, however, had any interest in denying the basic truths of Christianity, for their interests lay precisely in extending those truths into new fields, cosmic evolution and worldwide politics. Here "liberal" means the freedom to see how tradition is expanded and vitalized by new situations.

So, the Catholic mind does not dismiss fundamentalism as religiosity, as a modern magic show, but ponders its theological convictions—the image of God, the view of the world, hopes for men and women—against a wider incarnation.

A Catholic Critique of Fundamentalism

We have already seen some elements of the Catholic response to fundamentalism in the previous chapters on psychology and Catholic critics. Ultimately the Catholic differences with fundamentalism come from the very nature of Christianity: from the good news of the incarnation, from the long history of the church, from experiences of interpreting Christianity from Iona to Java. This chapter, our central section, is not so much a rejection of fundamentalist search for faith and grace but a look at why Catholicism follows a different path.

God in Creation and People

There is only one God. This God is both the creator of the universe, including the planet earth and human beings, and the redeemer of the human race. The God who fashioned the galaxies turned the execution of Jesus caused by political and religious leaders to the redemption of humanity. As creator and redeemer this God is more deeply committed to our good than we are. Thomas Aquinas says that creation and redemption come from an overflowing goodness in God, so vital that it cannot resist reaching out to other.[2] God's universe implies a divine intelligence while God's presence in our lives bespeaks love. This God permits evil but has no involvement with the sins we freely choose.

For Catholics, God is not an unpredictable trickster who might upset the laws of physics or the aspirations of humans just to dazzle. God is not a magician for whom nature and human life are simply a backdrop, stage or audience for the miraculous. Nor is God a demanding judge of wandering humanity, a universal hater of his own creation. Finally God is not presented in the New Testament as the director of an apocalyptic end of the world in fire and suffering engulfing innocent beings. Certainly, in the parables of Jesus' teaching we do not meet any of these gods. To consider the one God of creation and redemption is to return to the psychological and theological image of God, only to reject again the God of anger and fear. God's plans exist to serve us.

Fundamentalist attention to the things of religion has as its other side a fear of all else. Fundamentalism is somewhat world-hating, for it sincerely believes that a human being is largely sinful, that the world is more evil than good, and that everything outside of its own words is dangerous or demonic. When creation, human culture, is bad, one had best avoid the world, withdraw from cultures and societies, religions and philosophies. Since everything other than biblical phrases is evil, one is easily "infected" by art, science, life and history. If salvation is so narrow and God so strict, one might easily make a fatal mistake about which religious words are correct. Hating the world has its advantages: it calms anxiety by rejecting a list of forbidden things and people. Before the condemnation of billions, the fundamentalist becomes a star.

For Catholics, although they can cause many social and personal evils, men and women are basically good. Human reason is not suspect; freedom will not, when left ungoverned by laws and fear, always choose evil. Potential for good lies in the individual and in the society. Great societies and cultures, despite their deficiencies, are witnesses to the invention and transcendence of the human spirit.

Grace does not silence or cloak human nature; God's salvation does not replace our humanity, nor is human nature—baptized or unbaptized—something shameful, hated by its creator. Unlike fundamentalists, Catholics do not think a human person is tricky, corrupt, untrustworthy or ugly. Nor are the cultures of history with their art and religion products of the demonic. Grace draws each man and woman to an individualized destiny.

Ordinary Grace

Catholicism believes in a real revelation, in a true incarnation of God in a human being. Grace is a power and reality in our lives. The Bible is the special record of a divine history. Genesis states that men and women were made in the image and likeness of God. Thomas Aquinas interpreted this image to mean first our intellect and free will and then our acceptance of God's special presence, one lying deeper than the life of body and soul. God loves us with a new life and a special destiny. This life Jesus called the "kingdom of God" and Aquinas dares to see it as "friendship" from God, or a "share in the life of the Trinity."

Catholicism differs from fundamentalism in that it views God's presence in history and in our lives as being, most of the time, ordinary. Grace, Aquinas says, is "a special love of God" deeply but freely influencing our life. This presence of God is silent, active, unobtrusive even as it leads us to eternal life. Certainly there are prophetic figures—Elijah or Catherine of Siena, Francis of Assisi or Martin Luther King—but most Christians act out the decades of their lives in a silent dialogue with God. They believe and hope in his love but do not see proofs of it in miracles of healing or in financial gain. The saints of Catholicism exist not to witness to miracles but to illustrate divine life in men and women. Curiously, with all of its saints and shrines, Catholicism is very slow to acknowledge the miraculous. In its view of grace, most of the time God works in people powerfully but invisibly.

Fundamentalism demands the extraordinary. The miraculous proves the truth of this evangelist's church. Ordinary people are outsiders—perhaps even, in their ordinariness, the damned. An evangelist imagines that he alone in 1955 or 1985 in rural Tennessee has grasped Christianity. Sadly, a consequence of fundamentalism's elitism and apocalypticism is the easy decision that most men and women suffer an eternal punishment. Before an angry God, those who don't own an English Bible have no chance!

We enter and live in Jesus' reign and Spirit by *faith*. Jesus' kingdom really exists, and faith is our contact with this unseen, deeper reality. Faith for Catholics is not fantastic beliefs, a power for miracles, a set of religious words. Faith is not sustained by miracles but by daily life.

Faith offers a perspective on life. Not so much a detailed cerebral knowledge of heavenly beings and situations, belief is a look into our real situation as God sees it. Ideas about God, morality and revelation will express our faith, but faith lies deeper in our person. Faith means the risked acceptance that there is something more than the laws of physics and the daily reports from banking. There is a special presence of God over and above (or beneath) society and creation. Faith is an acceptance that there is "more." This "more" is grace, God's special presence on earth.

For the Catholic, faith and religion are always about something real. Faith, although it cannot see its objects (God, grace, love) is, nonetheless, not information about heaven, not an introverted psychology or a desperate hope, but access to "the real world." This orientation toward the tangible and the real unseen can lead to attitudes towards statues and grottos which are nourished more by superstition than by faith. Nonetheless, faith does not stop with ancient Greek creeds about Jesus or "the power of positive thinking." Faith is a way of seeing my life amid two forces: God's and evil's. This world is unseen, yet more real than the laws of gravity.

Thus faith and grace are about the ordinary. In a dark but firm commitment, faith gives access to the world of God's love toward us. This love comes not at our whims to interfere with the course of nature and history but in a manner of silent revelation and goodness for each human being.

Wide Grace

Jesus preached not expensive sacrifices to bribe a capricious god but the Trinity's plan and activity in us. Catholicism emphasizes the reality and importance of what we do with grace—but grace belongs to God. Christianity proclaims an access to God's realm which is for all men and women, universal and intimate. God is not a judge or an idol but the parent who goes out into the hot, dusty road to welcome the adult son or daughter who has wasted a fortune. God's grace is ordinary, too, because it is open to all (universal) and always present to us (even during our sinful turning away from it). We do not need to be holy or odd, a European Christian or a white male, to get God's attention. Nor do we need to proclaim our difference from others, discourse endlessly on the correctness of our theology and wear some religious piece of cloth or tin. God's silent conversation with us is more valuable and powerful than working a miracle or raising millions precisely because it goes beyond tribal religion to reach all. Fundamentalism, with its narrowness of salvation and generosity in condemnation, is almost pre-Christian. It is indeed "old time religion" because it is tribal religion from the past.

Catholic tradition holds that grace as the inviting, intimate presence of God on earth is not tied to the three "Bs": baptism, belief, belonging to a church. While faith in the gospel and membership in the church are the central ways of God's grace working in history overall, grace exists outside Christianity. Christ died for all men and women, not just for a small, select group predestined by an unpredictable and unpleasant deity millions of years ago. Although Jesus Christ is the unique, intense center and cause of grace, the presence celebrated by Christmas, Good Friday and Easter contacts all men and women in the silence of their lives and in their own religions. Here too Catholicism is the opposite of a fundamentalism which proclaims the landslide of most people—God's images—into hell.

Grace is present ecumenically in the family of Christian churches. Catholics, however, also acknowledge the presence of grace in the world religions. People outside of baptism and belief in Christ are not cut off from grace. While Christians believe Christ is the center of the history of religion, God is not so stingy with grace that the billions who have never known Christ are, without any fault of theirs, destined to be without grace forever. This is something fundamentalists find shocking.

Catholics use the word "grace" more frequently than faith. Faith is the intellectual perception and acceptance of Jesus' teaching. Grace—all that the kingdom of God implies—is a divine activity working invisibly in people. This non-elitist theology of grace permits Catholicism to be a church of many hundreds of millions in various cultures. God's presence comes to us in degrees within and outside the church. The incarnation, very special in Jesus, lives on not mainly in television shows, papal court ceremonies or miracles, but in us—in people living out a long history in a large church. We meet grace, begun and given by Jesus Christ, in the sacraments, in people, in the church and in daily life (whether we be accountants or Trappist monks). Just as Jesus was incarnate in a particular time and culture, so other cultures and times (not just Rome of the first century, Gaul of the fourth century, or America of the twentieth century) provide the body for the incarnation of the gospel and the sacraments. Thousands of languages can bring new ways of describing God's plan in Jesus, and the dramas of Asian self-understanding or the colors of African art and dances can incarnate baptism and eucharist.

Against the Neuroses of Religion

Jesus of Nazareth was not easily roused to criticism, but one area which called forth emotional condemnations and calls for reform was *religion.* Jesus did not become angry at sexual sin or at religious disinterest, but he is recorded as becoming angry over religion. He rejected religion as a superficial collection of externals, as words or rituals separate from inner honesty and generosity, as a buying and selling of God's favor. Jesus frequently criticized religion. In the last analysis, his religion, the Jewish religion, stands for all religion. He was vocal about religion used to injure people in the name of God and he bemoaned the violent distortions human beings have substituted for their relationships with God in the name of "religion." Woody Allen observes in one of his films: "If Jesus came back to earth and saw what people do in his name, he would throw up."

Why is Jesus interested in religion? Why is God interested in religion? We imagine that "religion" is God's enterprise or hobby, God's domain. Don't religion and God go together? In fact, God, the creator, is interested in all of creation and human life; the word of God is attracted by a trout leaping in the sunset or by the modulation of a sonata by Haydn. God is interested in religion because in religion God's relationship to us is discussed and furthered. Religion has a tremendous potential for good, and for evil. Religion is where my image of God and my image of being a man or a woman meet. What greater power for good (or for evil) than to invoke this belief or that policy as God's special will.

Jesus' preaching clearly intended to make men and women critical, in a deep sense, of religion. Jesus questioned religious forms. Were they superstition, magic? Were they childish or hypocritical? Were they faithful to the true life and plan of the kingdom of God? In an extraordinary way, far from identifying himself with the bazaar of religious hucksters, he understood that religion can have a healthy or a neurotic appeal. He challenged the unhealthy masks of religion. All of this is quite central for examining any fundamentalism, because it can substitute religion for faith, externals for grace. Like Jesus and his Spirit, religion serves the true God and the true human being.

We can see in Jesus' critique three unhealthy deformities of religion: elitism, fetishism, compulsion. All three are deeply entrenched in human religion; men and women may enter religion not out of love of God or hope in the future but to calm neuroses. *Elitism* means that religion gives me the conviction that I am better than other people—not just that I am loved by God, or that I am capable of loving people, but that religion stamps me permanently and loftily with a divine approval disdaining others. Belonging to a divinely approved group gives an identity which the individual cannot find alone, while a compulsion fulfilled (this form of prayer) brings a feeling of worth, of salvation. *Fetishism* invests some thing (a book, a medal, a religious phrase) with a divine presence and power too strong and too certain. *Compulsion* is the active side of the fetish: a relentless God demands that this or that action be done to avoid feelings of unworthiness.

The New Testament frequently describes Jesus struggling against and beyond elitism, fetishism and compulsion in religion. He avoids these three as he responded to the three questions with which men and women challenged him: Who is better? (The one who actually serves others!) What must I do? (Love others!) Who enters the kingdom of God? (Everyone who chooses, aided by grace, to enter the kingdom!) Behind these questions lie the unspoken interests: What is the minimum needed for God's favor? How do I get to be better than others? Jesus would rather not answer the questions posed, for by so doing he could appear to enter into the neurotic argument over this or that theological nuance or ritual. Don't they request a bottom-line list of religious requirements? In fact, we know the answer to these questions: our belief must accept God's special presence in my life; my activity must serve that dialogue in myself and others; all are called to this conversation, this kingdom, silently by the generous love of God. Those entering the kingdom of God are told that service is its style, its attitude toward other people. If we wish to be first, let us take ourselves to the true arena where religion is tested: the crossroads of needy humanity. At the end of a day of hard work among those who have nothing and need everything, who themselves can be neurotic and ungracious, who live in dirt and mediocrity, we will have lost our energy for scheming to be first.

History

The Catholic Church is old. The papacy is the oldest institution in the west; the Dominican Order to which this author belongs was two centuries old when the renaissance began, five and a half centuries old when the American constitution was written. There have been and are various theologies in Christianity: Roman and Ethiopian, Russian and Lutheran, Irish and Persian. There are different theologies within Catholicism: Jesuit and Franciscan approaches, theologies inspired by Aristotle or by Hegel. Catholicism strives for a gospel which is clear in its essentials but also capable of living in different cultures. The church with its movements and liturgies should be a multi-colored spectrum reaching from Chile to Nigeria.

Catholicism takes the long view. The Catholic Church expects the world to change slowly and has learned too that cultures become Christian slowly. A sudden confession of faith is not the same as a lifetime of practice.

History is the great enemy of every fundamentalism. History with its failures and successes, its different epochs read in books and seen in art, can appear to relativize religion. History, too, is a disappointment, for history is a record of theme and variation showing both sameness and difference. Governments under Marcus Aurelius, Richelieu, and Roosevelt had similar problems, but the forms are different. Would the church of early Rome recognize the church of the baroque? And yet, the same scriptures, the same sacraments, were venerated in both.

But time's diversity is not indifference or relativism. History illustrates how things both perdure and change, and, more painfully, that no one era has everything. Before history's dramas a man, a woman, becomes human, becomes wise.

History shows there is no golden age! But fundamentalism is intent upon recapturing a past golden age and upon condemning other periods as inferior or apostate. When the televangelists broadcast from Europe, their programs are arranged so that one gains the impression that Europe has never been Christian, that emptiness or sin existed between Paul in Rome at the time of Nero and the twentieth century. American preachers imply that they have regained or restored the gospel against numerous superstitions. The Benedictine abbeys or Jesuit schools in countries throughout the world, now and in the past, must be blocked out, for they imply zeal and wisdom in other lands at other times. The fundamentalist personality views the beautiful and painful diversity of human life as a danger, even a scandal. Fundamentalisms speak as if they had just discovered God and his revelation to people. They act as if God is absent or has been asleep until someone in rural Tennessee finds him. Since Jesus' Spirit came at Pentecost two thousand years ago, it is unlikely that the first inspired interpreter of the gospel and Spirit appeared only in 1920 or 1980. The true God is always active, universally present, incarnate not to condemn people but to save them.

The fundamentalists' enthusiasm for a violent end of the world goes together with their nervousness over diversity. Since history shows struggle and variety and since church history spotlights this American sect as a newcomer, the end of the world is welcome. The imminent approach of doom is a drama aimed at distracting people from the slow process of God's kingdom on earth, from the variety of peoples and eras incarnating the gospel. If you are angry at your world and ignorant of how the world of grace works, you desire the end of the cosmos.

Catholics should not be distracted by recent fundamentalisms of whatever brand from the larger role on earth of Christianity. What is the good news, the gospel? It is that the ongoing incarnation of Christ and his Spirit in ordinary life is the good news. Christianity affirms not a narrowminded God, but a savior who is both word of God and a real human being. This brother does not condemn but invites in various levels of belief and love the entire world to enter what touches and what is preached to all men and women: the kingdom of God.

Diversity in Life

History brings diversity. A Catholic critique of fundamental-ism is a critique based upon centuries of church history where not all theologies and practices of Christianity are the same. Different times and peoples, different languages and arts, have expressed Christianity in different ways. Circles of theologies and practices move around the center of the incarnation. It is not difficult to learn from the New Testament what is central (curiously fundamental-isms often omit areas important in the New Testament such as eucharist). We should not imagine that every Old Testament prophecy is on the same level as the sermon on the mount, or that a nincteenth century hymn equals baptism. There are different fami-lies of faith within Christian history and the Catholic Church.

The healthy believer can distinguish levels of faith, theology, practice, church life. The description of the clothes which wrapped the corpse of Jesus in the tomb are not of equal import with the promise of the Holy Spirit by the risen Christ. The church's pro-gram for society's poor is more significant than the number of candles or the fear of women active in the liturgy. A rigid personal-ity tends to give everything equal value; a fear-filled personality worries about any omission lest God be insulted. So the ability to join diversity with fidelity to church life and gospel is difficult for the fundamentalist mind.

Everything we have said about history is true of cultural diver-sity. In the black and white movies of the 1940s (of which *Raiders of the Lost Ark* is an enjoyable parody) cultures and religions other than Anglo-American Protestantism were treated not just as bizarre, perhaps superstitious and dirty, but as demonic. The camera depicted Egyptian, African or Asian religions as tribal dances or grotesque temples of doom and deviltry. All this flows from a fundamentalist view of the world: other races and other religions are not just different; they are evil. For Catholicism, cultures have good and bad sides, but each can be open to, actively receptive of, a new incarnation of grace and gospel.

Diversity exists because words do not fully capture realities. The tree is not the same as my mental idea of it or the English word "tree." Words are never things, never perfect representations. Jesus neither owned nor wrote a Bible. He preaches not about the right words or sacred things but about God's plan for men and women. The words of the Bible, of church decrees, of a sermon can illumine the deeper reality of God's secret conversation with me, but they do not imprison it.

God's presence within me is not tied to words printed in black and white or broadcast in color. We should distinguish between God's grace and the forms that grace uses. An evangelist is not God, nor is God's grace tied to a printed page, to water or to a particular hall. The forms of faith are important—the sacraments and words of Christianity are not arbitrary—but, without being secular or relativistic, we must be able to comprehend how God's grace is free. As new ideas, social structures and arts emerge, God's grace and the church's life are mature enough to work through them. Divine love can also act outside of these forms and contact us even when these forms do not communicate well his grace. In modern society, the church is interpreter and sign of the kingdom of God, but God's grace works in people and movements in society too.

The demands of morality and politics are real; culture and science always bring new problems. There are not always simple answers. Precisely the buildings and rituals of churches and religions through centuries, the variety of customs and cuisines, the stages of a single life—these threaten to asphyxiate the fundamentalist who has made such efforts to find the pure air of simplicity. But it is hard, on the other hand, for a Roman Catholic to live outside of ethnic diversity. A Catholic who dislikes history and fears diversity is disavowing tradition. To be a Catholic is to live in the tension of commitment to dogmatic truth and easy acceptance of diverse church languages and devotions.

Diversity and history point to the future. The future of Catholicism does not lie in the interpretation of a biblical passage, an apologetic syllogism or taxation on alcohol. Roman Catholicism, because of its commitment to a stable ethic, has to deal with the flood of new bio-medical issues; because of the church's presence in eastern Europe and Latin America, it must address the theories of Marx; because there are over a hundred million African Catholics, views of the spiritual life and of liturgy drawing on the myriad cultures of that continent must be developed. This is the future of grace rejoicing in diversity.

Humor

Some televangelists rarely smile; some always smile. The smiles that do come across the airwaves seem artificial. A reward for contributions?

Humor laughs through the ambiguity in life. Where there is certitude, rigidity, or fear there is little humor. If human nature is corrupt, if the world is worthy of destruction, laughter seems improper. Anyone who has talked to Protestant or Catholic, Californian or Libyan fundamentalists knows that there is no appreciation of humor. In humor limits are transcended or not observed (there are funny jokes about death); humor is often self-deprecating and involves the implicit confession that we don't know everything. Humor is angelic because in jokes we surpass for a moment our human condition. We laugh instead of weep about its pains; we smilingly hope in the future. But won't humor make people slack, encourage a lack of seriousness before God? Humor might be a trojan horse containing within what is not orthodox.

There is nothing funny within fundamentalist religion. Its visions of salvation are fragile shelters in a world of sinners destined for fire. So strict, it reveals no exceptions to the rules. Seeking stardom and elitism, it cannot embrace the democracy of laughter. Some human beings cannot imagine anything being funny about the mind of God, and humor relativizes absolutes.

The ethnic diversity of Catholicism joined to the tragic history of its immigrant populations in the past century encourages humor. Since God cannot be enclosed fully in a human being, an incarnational perspective will catch the pomposities of the human pretending to be divine. There is some truth to the parodies of Moses' fifteen (that is, ten!) commandments or the Spanish Inquisition in Mel Brooks' *History of the World,* and to the relentless religiosity of *Saturday Night Live's* Church Lady.

Perhaps the ultimate anecdote of religious humor comes from Teresa of Avila. St. Teresa spent her life as a mystic in a monastery of nuns, but circumstances drew her to establish a reform of the Carmelite Order. This involved many difficulties. Traveling on a mission filled with disappointments, her donkey cart, during a downpour, became stuck, and then, through efforts to free it, turned over spilling the riders into the mud. Teresa, at an end of patience, complained inwardly to Jesus. She then felt conscious of an answer from the Lord to whom all her work was dedicated: "But you see, Teresa: this is how I treat my friends." Teresa spontaneously replied: "Then, Lord, no wonder that you have so few." This extraordinary woman, gifted in both prayer and politics, gives us one of the few occasions when a person has the last word on the word of God.

Ultimately the differences between Catholics and fundamentalists are simple but profound: (1) Who is God and how does God act toward us? (2) Who are we—basically evil creatures, potential miracle workers, or persons seeking our special identity? (3) How do men and women, through history, life and culture, receive and then act alone and in community under God's grace?

Every fundamentalism (including Catholics who have made a fundamentalism of a few aspects of their church) will be shocked at the Roman Catholic Church.

Catholicism lives out of the supernatural presence of God in history. It expects the revelation of the New Testament to become flesh and blood in the languages of all nations. While it affirms on rare occasion the possibility of the miraculous, it views grace as ordinary and universal. Catholicism is worldwide, and so it cannot espouse just one form of faith and worship. Catholicism knows a great deal about human sin. Experience has made it wise concerning the potential for evil lying deep in all men and women. This Christian approach in theory never espouses relativism, but in practice it distinguishes levels of human behavior and forgives every sin while understanding that not every failing should be broadcast. But the meaning of grace-in-history permits it to expect future saints in every race, to look for social renewal in every country.

Conclusion

"Humanity is sleeping—it is still sleeping—imprisoned in the narrow joys of its closed loves. Jesus, Savior of human activity to which you have given meaning, compel us to discard our pettinesses, and to venture forth, resting upon you, into the uncharted ocean of charity."

PIERRE TEILHARD DE CHARDIN

What separates Catholics from fundamentalism? It is not arguments over biblical texts disapproving of calling anyone "Father," nor apocalyptic prophecies emanating from Iranian clerics, nor news reports on Channel 11 on how many miracles occurred yesterday morning. Rather, as the preceding short chapters have shown, theological, psychological and cultural disagreements distinguish Catholicism from evangelical–fundamentalist interpretations of Christianity. All of these touch upon one issue: What does it mean to be a human being who is also a citizen of the kingdom of God?

Catholicism exists in the sacramental middle. It lies between a liberalism which has no ethical certainties and no faith in revelation in history, and a myriad of fundamentalisms. The sacramental milieu is not the same as a middle position on doctrinal issues, nor is it a realm of mediocrity. The sacramental milieu is not theologies or middle positions at all, but the appearance of the ordinariness of grace and the dignity of our identity. The grace and teaching of Jesus overflow beyond a book or a conversion (or, for Catholic fundamentalists, a logic or a medal) into liturgy, celebration, politics and social service. In this multiple and colorful sacramentality, art and dogma, politics and athletics, ethnicity and mysticism are all at home. Thus Catholicism in the theology school and at the parish picnic is the opposite of the monoform, the sectarian and the fundamentalist.

Catholic theologies and practices occur in the forms and ideas of a dozen cultures. On Easter night, fires are ignited, candles are plunged into pools of water—strange practices! Mediterranean Catholicism is not puritan, and yet includes communities of celibate monks and hermits. The Catholic Church is large and moves slowly; fundamentalisms are small and can be born, regroup and die very quickly (as the recent history of PTL illustrates).

Protestant and Catholic fundamentalisms frequently attack or ignore Vatican II. Why? Vatican II was an event of change—it marked the end of four centuries of an absence of change and the beginning of a post-conciliar period of vitality and newness. The council is also an act of historical transition. Looking at the pastoral needs of the times it discerned what is permanent in belief and liturgy and what should be changed so that the church can breathe and expand. Parish life should suit generations alive now; theology is for the living, not the dead. The council ended the dull and inaccurate rejection of modern life without embracing secularity or lukewarm faith. The council accepted critically the aspirations of the world and realized that the church could not speak to this century and the next in languages long antiquated. A fundamentalism will reject Vatican II because Vatican II is the affirmation not of a God isolated in heaven, cathedral or printed page but of the Trinity at work on earth precisely through history and change, through diversity born of pastoral concern for people.

Catholicism is in the process of becoming truly worldwide, in the process of becoming more than European and baroque. It has been, except for its semitic roots and early churches, largely European, and Catholicism has not changed much from the middle ages, or even from the end of the Roman empire. With Vatican II it was summoned to be worldwide, to permit Jesus to be interpreted as a prophet among the poor of Latin America, to encourage liturgies suited to the Cameroons, spiritualities for India.

The opposite of "catholic" and "worldwide" is sectarian. The sect interprets grace's presence narrowly, theologically views the world as evil, and ecclesiastically tends to exclude rather than include. Sectarianisms and fundamentalisms—whether they be of Protestant or Catholic origin, of political or theological direction—are perhaps the great threat to Roman Catholicism in the United States in the period following Vatican II. This is why a touchstone of controversy with fundamentalism is the belief that while all grace is centered in Christ, grace can exist outside of Bible, baptism and belief. Grace, most explicit in Christ, can exist in men and women of other cultures and religions pursuing their own God-given identity in the midst of the real worlds of sin and offered grace. Fundamentalism holds that all outside are damned—a world of difference!

Fundamentalism is always the same: the same psychological needs, the same exclusion of any new idea or movement. The rigidity of a fundamentalism ultimately spells, despite every success, its limitations and decline, for it cannot adapt or deal with pluralism. It remains a sect, a small group of religious elite. It has a short-term future but no wide audience (as much as the television transmitters strain to cover the globe), for it has no potential for diversity. Thus in the space of a few generations, each fundamentalism, if it continues, dies and starts again. A new evangelist begins Christianity all over again, with the same exaggerated claims, and with the same global condemnations of the past and present.

In contrast to the parade of well-advertised and self-confident fundamentalists there arises a choir of figures whose life and thought have been dedicated to the contemplation of how God's presence enters human life slowly and quietly: Thomas Aquinas with his harmony of personality and grace; Teresa of Avila with her common sense and elevation of faith over the miraculous; Thomas Merton, contemplative without being isolationist, prophetic without being condemnatory; Pope John XXIII welcoming all of good will toward the reforming power of the Holy Spirit; Teilhard de Chardin sketching how all of evolution is empowered by and destined for the future Christ.

Religious things are not the absolute; the absolute is God's Spirit in men and women. We will avoid fundamentalisms if we avoid investing things with magic rather than sacramental power, if we do not confuse a series of Latin, Greek or English words with the revelation of God. Finally, the Son of God came not to condemn the injured and the ignorant but to show God's true self, mercy and love. If Jesus is our advocate, our savior and our deacon, then human beings should be slow to assume more drastic roles of judge and magician. Like the mentor of God's plan to us, Jesus Christ, church and Bible, prophet and charismatic, bishop and teacher— everything in the reign of God—aim at service. As Meister Eckhart, the great medieval Dominican mystic, wrote: "This is why scripture was written, why the world was created, why angels and people exist; that God might be born in us, and that we might be born in God."

Coming out from buildings in the great cities of the world we are called to accept mysteries that are beyond dogma. We do not fully understand God's plan for earth, but we know its dynamics and structure in Jesus' preaching about the reign of God. We do not know how Jesus crucified and risen is the center of the long and colorful history of human religion, but we know that his union with the word of God gives him a definitive position. But around us, in the streets of Lagos, Los Angeles or Istanbul, are men and women who receive God's grace rather than condemnation, and who deserve our respect and love. Their lives in their religions, as well as the diversity of Christian traditions, call forth hope and faith in presence of Christ on earth, a power and word perhaps just beginning.

Notes

1. Fundamentalism and Our Times

[1] *Beyond Fundamentalism* (Philadelphia, 1984), ix.
[2] "Fundamentalism: A Pastoral Concern," *The Bible Today* (1983), 1.
[3] Jimmy Swaggart, *The Lord Jesus Christ, Salvation, The Holy Bible, and Roman Catholicism* (Baton Rouge, 1985); cf. also *A Letter to My Catholic Friends* (Baton Rouge, 1986).
[4] "Defection Among Hispanics," *America* 157 (July 30, 1988), 61ff.
[5] *Listen America* (Toronto, 1980), 12.
[6] "Fundamentalism," 1.
[7] "Fundamentalism," 2.
[8] J.F. Whealon, "Fighting Fundamentalism," *America* 154 (October 12, 1985), 211.
[9] *Beyond Fundamentalism,* viii.
[10] *Beyond Fundamentalism,* ix.
[11] "Fundamentalism," 4.

2. Catholic Fundamentalisms

[1] "Who Are the Catholic 'Fundamentalists'?" *Commonweal* 116 (1989), 47. For a survey of this movement, cf. D. Menozzi, "Opposition to the Council (1966–1984)," *The Reception of Vatican II* (Washington, 1987), 325ff.
[2] Patrick Arnold, "The Rise of Catholic Fundamentalism," *America* 156 (1987), 297.
[3] "The Rise of Catholic Fundamentalism," 298.
[4] "The Rise of Catholic Fundamentalism," 306.

[5] "The Rise of Catholic Fundamentalism," 306.
[6] "The Rise of Catholic Fundamentalism," 306.
[7] "The Rise of Catholic Fundamentalism," 306.
[8] Peter Hebblethwaite, "A Roman Catholic Fundamentalism," *Times Literary Supplement* (August 5–11), 1988, 866.
[9] "A Roman Catholic Fundamentalism," 866.
[10] *An Introduction to Christian Faith* (New York, 1980), 144ff.
[11] "The Rise of Catholic Fundamentalism," 305. A second group, solely American, is analyzed by M. Timothy Iglesias, "CUF and Dissent. A Case Study in Religious Conservatism," *America* 156 (1987), 303ff. He observes there a lack of historical understanding of theology, a focus upon an inner renewal which will avoid liturgical or political issues, a challenge to episcopal authority, and a militant campaign to remove, at any price, teachers it finds objectionable. Curiously, despite these "faults", the author concludes by noting the "careful leadership and good will" of a "legitimate" Catholic group (307).

3. A False Ecumenism

[1] A. Carey, "Catholic College Students Lured by Fundamentalists," *Our Sunday Visitor* (April 5, 1987), 3; cf. K. Keating, *Catholicism and Fundamentalism* (San Francisco, 1988).
[2] Cf. T.F. O'Meara, "The End of Liberal Theology," *The Lutheran Quarterly* 23 (1971), 268ff.

4. The Psychology of Fundamentalism

[1] *Beyond Fundamentalism* (Philadelphia, 1984), 174.
[2] *Does God Exist? An Answer for Today* (New York, 1980), 676.
[3] *Evangelism in America. From Tents to TV* (New York, 1988), 167.
[4] "Where To Find Answers To Religious Questions?" *The Catholic Transcript* (June 13, 1986), 5.
[5] *Images of Hope: Imagination as the Healer of the Hopeless* (New York, 1965), 214.

[6] *Seeds of Contemplation* (New York, 1949), 26f.

[7] *Seeds of Contemplation,* 27.

5. Catholic Critics

[1] "Threat of Catholic Fundamentalism," *The Catholic Transcript* (July 26, 1985), 5.

[2] "Threat of Catholic Fundamentalism," 5.

[3] "Proper Interpretation Key to Understanding," *The Catholic Transcript* (August 9, 1985), 5. McBrien is referring to the declaration *Mysterium Ecclesiae* issued in 1973 by the Congregation for the Doctrine of the Faith. See also McBrien's columns for September 27, 1985, October 4, 1985, and October 11, 1985 as printed in *The Catholic Transcript.*

[4] The following quotations are drawn from "Roman Catholicism: *E Pluribus Unum,*" *Daedalus* 111 (1982), 73ff. For a larger systematic unfolding of the three principles, cf. *Catholicism* (Minneapolis: Winston, 1980).

[5] The following quotations are drawn from K.D. Rucker, "The Bible, the Church and Fundamentalism: An On-the-Run Talk with Raymond Brown," *St. Anthony Messenger* 93 (December 1983), 11ff.

[6] The following quotations are taken from "Pastoral Statement for Catholics on Biblical Fundamentalism," *Origins* 17 (1987), 376f.

[7] *Mystery and Manners* (New York, 1969), 118.

[8] *Wise Blood* (New York, 1962), 105, 113.

[9] "The Teaching of Literature," cited in R. Coles, *Flannery O'Connor's South* (Baton Rouge, 1980), 104.

[10] "Revelation," *The Complete Short Stories* (New York, 1985), 502, 507.

[11] "Truth Flashes," *Commonweal* 113 (1986), 678.

[12] "Truth Flashes," 678.

[13] "The Lame Shall Enter First," *The Complete Stories,* 480.

[14] "Revelation," *The Complete Stories,* 508.

[15] "The Fiction Writer and His Country," *Collected Works* (New York, 1988), 805.

[16] Letter to John Hawkes (1959) cited in R. Coles, *Flannery O'Connor's South,* 59.

6. The Catholic Perspective

[1] *Beyond Fundamentalism* (Philadelphia, 1984).

[2] Thomas Aquinas, *Summa theologiae* III, q. 1, a. 1.

Bibliography

B. Altenmeyer, *Enemies of Freedom. Understanding Right-Wing Authoritarianism* (San Francisco, 1988).

P.M. Arnold, "The Rise of Catholic Fundamentalism," *America* 156 (April 11, 1987), 297ff.

J. Barr, *Fundamentalism* (Philadelphia, 1977).

———, *Beyond Fundamentalism* (Philadelphia, 1984).

R.J. Bater, "Fundamentalism and the Parish," *Church* 4 (1988), 7ff.

K.C. Boone, *The Bible Tells Them So. The Discourse of Protestant Fundamentalism* (Ithaca, 1988).

L. Caplan, *Studies in Religious Fundamentalism* (Ithaca, 1984).

John A. Coleman, "Who Are the Catholic 'Fundamentalists'?" *Commonweal* 116 (January 27, 1989), 42ff.

Thomas Coskren, "Fundamentalists on Campus," *New Catholic World* 228 (1985), 38ff.

E. Dobson, "Fundamentalism—Its Roots," *New Catholic World* 228 (1985), 4ff.

L. Foley, "Catholics and Fundamentalists: We Agree and Disagree," *St. Anthony Messenger* 91 (July 1983), 15ff.

———, *Catholic Update: How Should Catholics View Fundamentalism?* (Cincinnati, 1983).

R. Gaillardetz, "The Challenge of the Evangelicals," *Pastoral Life* 34 (1985), 2ff.

A. Giles, *Fundamentalism: What Every Catholic Needs To Know* (Cincinnati, 1984).

J. Higgins, "A Catholic Look at Fundamentalism," *The Liguorian* 69 (1981), 48ff.

M.T. Iglesias, "CUF and Dissent. A Case Study in Religious Conservatism," *America* 156 (April 11, 1987), 303ff.

D. Kraus, "Catholic Fundamentalism: A Look at the Problem," *Living Light* 19 (1982), 8ff.

E. LaVerdiere, *Fundamentalism: A Pastoral Concern* (Collegeville, 1983).

———, "Fundamentalism and Christian Belief," *Emmanuel* 92 (October 1986), 424ff.

R. McBrien, "Religion and Politics in America, The 1988 Campaign," *America* 158 (May 28, 1988), 551ff.

———, *Catholicism* (Minneapolis, 1980).

S. Marrow, *The Words of Jesus in Our Gospels: A Catholic Response to Fundamentalism* (New York, 1979).

M. Marty, "Modern Fundamentalism," *America* 155 (September 27, 1986), 133ff.

D. Menozzi, "Opposition to the Council (1966–1984)," in G. Alberigo, ed., *The Reception of Vatican II* (Washington, 1987), 325ff.

T.F. O'Meara, "Fundamentalism and the Christian Believer," *The Priest* 44 (1988), 39ff.

K. Rucker, "The Bible, the Church and Fundamentalism: An On-the-Run Talk with Raymond Brown," *St. Anthony Messenger* 93 (December 1985), 11ff.

Thomas Stransky, "A Catholic Looks at American Fundamentalists," *New Catholic World* 228 (1985), 10ff.

J.F. Whealon, "Challenging Fundamentalism," *America* 154 (September 1985), 136ff.

L.J. White, "Fundamentalism and the 'Fullness of Christianity': Catholicism's Double Challenge," *Biblical Theology Bulletin* 18 (1987), 50ff.

Fundamentalists Anonymous (Video Cassette, 1986).

Pastoral Statement for Catholics on Biblical Fundamentalism, Origins 17:21 (November 5, 1987), 376ff.